Teaching
Stories

Teaching Stories

JUDY LOGAN

Afterword by Peggy McIntosh

TEACHING STORIES
Copyright © 1997 by Judy Logan
Afterword Copyright © 1997 by Peggy McIntosh
First edition published 1999 by Kodansha America Inc.

Second edition: 2013
ISBN: 978-1484917763

Cover photo by Jondou Chase Chen
Cover reviews courtesy of Kodansha America, Inc.

Book design by Jo-Anne Rosen
www.wordrunner.com/publish

Printed in the U.S.A. by createspace.com

To Peggy McIntosh

In loving memory of
Cathy Louise Nelson
1953 – 1998

Author's Note

The chapters of this book are organized thematically not chronologically. Some of the stories in this book took place before my sabbatical in 1990, others span my teaching career to its very beginning in 1966. These stories are true, but all student and parent names have been changed, as have some details of stories. Teachers Kathie Edeli, Jeanne Gallo, and Frank Foreman are real people, as are Suzanne O'Bryan and Felicia Lowe. The names of other teachers and school staff have been changed.

A word about tenses: I often start a story in the past tense because it happened a long time ago but then switch to the present tense to give the reader a sense of immediacy. This is deliberate and I hope it will not offend too many English teachers.

Contents

Introduction

On the day I opened the door to my classroom for the last time, I carried four bouquets of flowers with me to give away: beautiful spring flowers—daffodils, irises, roses, and lilies. I put them in a large vase filled with water, set them on the table among the packed boxes of books and materials, and thought about how I had come to be here, and what I was about to leave behind. The flowers were meant to be gifts of love and gratitude, meant to express what words cannot.

The first bouquet went to my friend Kathie, who shared my classroom for over twenty years. The second bouquet was for Peter, who has worked with Kathie and her students as a paraprofessional for many years. The third bouquet I gave to Frank Foreman, the Art, English, and Social Studies teacher who has co-directed the Gifted and Talented Education (GATE) Program with me for more than ten years.

The fourth bouquet of flowers I left for the classroom itself, as a tribute to all that had happened here. My history in this room is full and rich. I taught in this school for 24 years, and my mother, my uncle, my aunts, cousins, my sister and I had all been students here.

From my classroom window I could see the hospital where I was born. I could see the little house on Collingwood Street where my grandmother lived, and to which my parents brought me as an infant so that my mother could rest after childbirth and get used to being a new mother. I can see the back of the house on 19th and Douglass Streets where I grew up, and the house on 20th and Castro Streets where I live now. I looked out my classroom window and I saw my life.

My teaching has been deeply influenced by my experiences here. The stories in this book are the ones that best illustrate my own struggle to make my classroom a safe, comfortable, inspiring place for students of different backgrounds. These stories show people what it looks like to engage children in their own learning and what really happens when teachers and their students bring their lives into the classroom.

I was born in San Francisco in 1942, several blocks from the school I will call Dolores, where most of *Teaching Stories* takes place. I was the oldest of three daughters of working class parents, and my maternal grandparents were Norwegian immigrants who came to San Francisco around the turn of the century.

When I was a little girl, I loved listening to my mother tell me stories of her childhood. She seemed to have had such freedom, exploring the city with her friends and brothers and sisters, sometimes taking the ferry across the bay, then the train to the top of Mt. Tamalpais. I heard how she roller-skated up and down the hills of San Francisco, played baseball and soccer and kick-the-can with her neighborhood friends, and spent time at the local library and public swimming pool.

As with many immigrant families, a sense of ethnicity defined our lives. My family attended the Norwegian Lutheran Church, a beautiful red-brick structure across the street from Dolores Park. At Christmastime we joined hands and sang Norwegian Carols as we circled the Christmas tree there. We went to wedding celebrations and holiday parties at a large meetinghouse purchased by the Sons and Daughters of

Norway. My own appreciation for and understanding of my personal history strengthened my commitment to encourage my students to explore and share their personal histories in the classroom.

In the 1930's, when my mother went to Dolores Junior High School, there were 1,500 seventh, eighth, and ninth graders in attendance. Students were offered courses in English, History, Math, Algebra, Geometry, General Science, Botany, Biology, Choral Music, Orchestra, Band, Art, Drama, French, Italian, Spanish, Latin, and German (taught by a "real professor with a goatee"). There was a special class called Conservation of Sight for students with eye problems. Immigrant children who did not yet speak English attended a newcomers' class for six months and were given intensive instruction in their new language.

Boys took woodshop, printing shop, and sheet metal shop. Girls took sewing and cooking classes. (Occasionally, my mother tells me, a boy would take a cooking class, but there was never a boy in any of her classes.) My mother took sewing for three years, and began making all her own clothes. Later, she would sew her own wedding dress and those of her bridesmaids. Twenty -six years later she did the same for me.

My own experiences at Dolores Middle School from 1953 to 1955 reflected my mother's in many ways. Many teachers there still remembered her. Like her, I walked the eleven blocks to and from school, up and down hills. Like her, I did well in school, made many friends.

I remember how nervous I was when I had to make a speech in front of the entire school. The huge auditorium was dark, so I couldn't see any faces, but as I sat on a chair on the stage, waiting my turn, my heart pounded so I thought I just might die. I don't think I have ever been as nervous since. Little did I know then that I would stand on that same stage and hand out diplomas for over twenty years.

As a student at Dolores Middle School I felt successful. I loved my classes and I loved my teachers. In English, Mr. Jensen sometimes let us work with our friends, (now we call it cooperative learning) and Julie and Virgie and I wrote a radio play based on the then-popular radio show, "The Shadow." We stood outside the classroom speaking and singing spookily into a large stand-up silver microphone, and managed to carry off our production without giggling. Mr. Jensen was also the first person to teach me about the history of the English language, and it was in his class that my future college major in English Literature and my minor in Language Arts was hatched. I assisted Mr. Grove, a shop teacher, with locker assignments, and I remember still how kind he was. Mr. Jones, my Social Studies teacher, took a photograph of me when I was in the seventh grade. I was president of the scholarship society when our class visited Sacramento, so I got to sit in the governor's chair and have my picture taken. Mr. Jones gave this framed photo to my parents when I left the school.

Although my mother attended one year of college, no one in my parents' families had ever graduated from college. Still, somehow my parents conveyed to me that there was no question but that I would go to college, and, in my mind, there was never a question that I would grow up to be a teacher. Since second grade, when I fell in love with the kindness of my instructor, Miss Miles, I had wanted to be a teacher. In the 1950's, this was the best career I could imagine for myself. Teaching was a traditional women's profession at that time, but in my family it was still traditional to be a homemaker.

In order to prepare me for college, my parents decided I should go to Lowell High School, a highly competitive college preparatory school that was then the only four- year high school in the city at the time. They also decided that I should leave Dolores Junior High at the end of the eighth grade and take advantage of all four years of high school. All of my friends stayed to finish the ninth grade and graduate. I was the only one to leave, and I knew no one in the ninth grade at Lowell. I was devastated to leave my friends and teachers, and for good reason, because my whole life changed. I was unprepared for a more ruthless, competitive philosophy of education, and I spent the first two years rebelling against it. Also, I experienced class issues in a different way, as I was now the underclass. Things that had seemed normal, or invisible to me, came into focus in a painful way as I sat in class in my homemade skirts with lots of starched crinolines and flowered print blouses amidst girls in their dyed-to-match cashmere sweaters and skirts. Eventually I pulled myself together and did well enough at Lowell to get into college, but by the time I got into San Francisco State, instead of sharing the joy and pride of my family, I felt like a failure, since most of my classmates were going to Stanford, Berkeley, or Ivy League Colleges in the East.

After I graduated from San Francisco State in 1964, I worked for a year, then took a government loan and returned to State to get my teaching credential. Nevertheless I learned a lot at San Francisco State, which had a wonderful English Department. I was in a two-semester student teaching program that encouraged us to have diverse experiences: one semester in a middle to upper class school, one semester in what was then called an underprivileged school; one semester in a high school, one semester in a junior high school. So I spent my first term teaching *Macbeth* to a gifted tenth grade class at Tamalpais High School in Marin County and I loved it. While I always knew I wanted to be a teacher, it wasn't until I taught that I realized how right this was for me. I can't explain this. I was a potter who had discovered clay, a swimmer in water, a gardener with her hands in dirt. At the end of my Shakespeare unit, I asked the students to write evaluations. I still have the one line comment from the boy who had been an outspoken and reluctant student: "Shakespeare finally made sense."

My second semester of student teaching was completely different. At Bayview Junior High School I was the only white person in my classroom. I wasn't the expert I thought I was. I had some students in my room who couldn't read and write, and I didn't know what to do about that. I couldn't remember how I had learned to read and write. Shakespeare was no help. And worst of all, many of these students didn't like school, didn't like me, sometimes didn't like themselves. Although I was offered a job at a school of high achieving, well-behaved students when I received my credential, Bayview was where I chose to stay, because it was where I had the most to learn. I had to learn how to teach reading, how to confront my own and others' racism, how to deal with violence, and how to expand my notion of teaching beyond the content of the curriculum.

So in 1966, while hundreds of flower children were streaming into San Francisco to celebrate free love, peace, drugs and hippie-dom, I was newly married and focused on my first year of teaching. Although I, too, marched against the Vietnam War and hoped for a better world, each morning I carefully dressed in comparatively conservative clothes (at that time female teachers were not allowed to wear pants or boots) in order to impress these students. One of the worse insults they could think of was to call someone a hippie. Having never been allowed into the middle class, my students had only contempt for those who rebelled against it.

Perhaps it was the spirit of the times, perhaps it was because

I was so young, perhaps it was simply my sense of values, but it was impossible for me to teach without becoming politically involved. When I started at Bayview, there was no parent/teacher association. Parents in general were not actively involved in the school. In fact, it seemed that administrators deliberately separated community and faculty, and I felt this could only hurt students. I joined about twelve other new teachers, and when we were unsuccessful in encouraging the faculty to develop a parent/teacher association, we began meeting with parents at the library on Third Street every Friday night. Many meetings and about four years later the school had its first African American principal, an active parent support group, and its first reading program. Most of what I know about teaching I learned those first few years. A few stories from these years appear at the end of this book. The four years I spent there were more instructional than my four years in college. But they were also difficult, discouraging years, and I finally requested a transfer.

The second job I was offered was at Dolores Junior High where my mother and I had been students. I felt like I was coming home. My students reminded me of myself, and every part of the school reminded me of my own experiences there. My mother's graduation picture was displayed in the library. There were still a few teachers there who remembered me. When I walked into the lobby for my interview with the principal, I had a deja vu experience where everything suddenly shifted down and looked as it had when I was four inches shorter. I remembered where my locker was, and which teacher was in each room. I remembered what the gym smelled like, and how dangerous it was to go to the bathrooms off the yard, where girls would threaten to beat you up if you were by yourself. I remembered how it felt to sit on the stage with my heart pounding. What would it be like to sit on the other side of the desk here? My parents gave me the picture of myself as a seventh grader, which had been taken by my teacher, and I hung it on my classroom wall, where for the next twenty four years it reminded me of myself as a student, and gave my students a glimpse of myself as an adolescent ("Ms. Logan, is that YOU?").

I was to teach English and Social Studies in a team-teaching situation to compensatory education students. Four teachers shared a classroom—the room that would eventually become "mine"—along with four paraprofessionals and about fifty-five children who were at least two to three years behind in reading. It was 1970 and there was a lot of money available for education. I had sixteen students for three periods in the morning, and sixteen students for three periods in the afternoon. We had a caring, structured program with high expectations for each student. The reading skills scores of some of these students came up three or four years while in our classroom. I liked the people I worked with, I liked my students, and I felt that what I was doing was important.

Back then the school had about 850 students. It was still a school with many immigrants, but by 1970 these newcomers came from Mexico, Central America, Southeast Asia, the Philippines, and Hong Kong. There was a large bilingual department for Spanish speaking, Tagalog-speaking, and Cantonese-speaking students as well as many ESL (English as a Second Language) classes. The school remained racially and economically mixed. Located in the center of San Francisco, the school drew from four diverse neighborhoods. Chicano, Latino, and Filipino students came from the east, the Mission District. Black students came from the north, the Fillmore. To the west is the largest gay/lesbian neighborhood in our city, the Castro, and we had some students from those families, and to the south came students from a mostly white, middle class neighborhood, Noe Valley. Students were bussed in from Treasure Island, a Navy base. Asian students came from the neighborhood and across town from Chinatown. Students from all over the city were in attendance because Dolores Middle School housed a Gifted and Talented Education Program known as GATE.

The education philosophy of the seventies encouraged team teaching and flexible scheduling; walls were being torn down. Teachers of different disciplines worked together to plan and implement curriculum centered on themes. What used to be two classrooms across from the principal's office became one large space for four teachers and one hundred students. Another two classrooms became one open area. Because my classroom was formerly the library, a very large space, with lots of bookshelves, we didn't have to tear down walls. All seventh grade students were in a Learning Center, with English, Social Studies, Math and Science teachers working together to plan and teach theme-based curricula. (Plans for such "family classes" are currently being discussed in the district as a nineties innovation.)

By 1970, too, boys and girls were taking the same electives. Students were programmed through introductory units in typing/computers, music, art, and shop. But sewing machines and cooking utensils were stored in the basement. Equal opportunity was perceived as girls "getting to" do traditional male activities, but traditional female activities were consciously or unconsciously perceived as no longer important, or inappropriate for boys. To make room for "equality," a whole department was dropped. It took me a long time to think seriously about the repercussions of this approach.

In 1979 there was a long teachers' strike in San Francisco. My friend, Deborah, who had been teaching in the GATE department, decided not to return to teaching after the strike was settled. I transferred into her job that year teaching English and Social Studies. For the next fifteen years, from 1979 to 1994, I taught in and eventually co-directed the GATE program. In San Francisco this program serves mostly academically talented students who test in the top two percent, or who score well in at least one area of the California Test of Basic Skills (CTBS), or whose teacher(s) recommend them for the program based on classroom behaviors (not necessarily positive behaviors — under-challenged students can be very difficult). After taking twelve units of classes to prepare for this specialized classroom, I began attending California Association of the Gifted (CAG) conferences, which presented many workshops on identifying gifted behaviors, motivating gifted children, and addressing their curriculum needs. Also in the early 1980s, our three-year program changed from seventh through ninth grades to sixth through eight grades. Dolores Junior High became Dolores Middle School.

Because I had been in the old library for so long, I was able to keep my room. Kathie Edeli, my friend and colleague, continued to teach Special Education Math and English classes at one end of the room, while I taught at the other. We liked it that when students walked into our room, people could not tell which special program they were in. Kathie, particularly, had fought hard not to have her small group of students relegated to a small corner of the school, tucked away in a closetlike classroom.

My relationships with many of the students portrayed in this book have blossomed into friendships, and we have kept in touch over the years. I often receive high school and university graduation announcements. I have been invited to Sweet Sixteen birthday parties, dance recitals, dramatic performances, bar mitzvahs, bat mitzvahs, New Year celebrations, graduation parties, and weddings. I have taught some of the children of my former students, making me a grandma teacher. Former students have been invited to my home as well. When I received the Eleanor Roosevelt grant from the American Association of University Women, I had an Eleanor Roosevelt tea party, attended by many students and parents and grandparents who had become friends.

I believe that a good teacher is passionately on the side of her students. That does not mean that I support them in everything they do. It means I demand the best from them and am willing to help them be their best selves. It means I listen, explain, support, and allow without judgment, sarcasm, or the need to impose truth from the outside in. The passage from childhood to adulthood that we call adolescence is a very vulnerable journey. It is often a difficult time for students and their families. It is an adolescent's "job" to rebel at times and to question the family environment that was such a comfortable cocoon during childhood. No matter how wonderful the parents, how loving the family, each adolescent needs to have other adults in whom to confide. If the family is the cathedral, I am the flying buttress, digging in my heels, leaning forward, stretching my arms out to the stone walls and throwing all my weight into helping the family reach for the skies. Being student-centered doesn't mean I am against parents or colleagues or administrators. It does mean I can sometimes treat the adolescent as the adult whom the parent does not yet see, the colleague may be still trying to control, the administrator may view as a threat ("What do you mean you don't want to salute the flag!"). Being student-centered doesn't mean I have an "anything goes" attitude toward my students. On the contrary, I have very high expectations for them, not only as future professionals, but also as creative and moral beings. While I have many enriching and affectionate relationships with colleagues, parents and administrators (my best friends are teachers), my deepest relationships are with my students.

Sarah Lawrence Lightfoot, a professor of education at Harvard's Graduate School of Education, says that we teachers need to see ourselves reflected in our students—we need to see them as our destiny, and the students need to see themselves in us. The faces of my students have changed since my mother's generation. The immigrants now are more likely to be from the Philippines, Hong Kong, Guatemala, Mexico, or El Salvador than from Italy, Germany, Norway or France. But the journey is similar, the experiences echo each other, and the welcome need be just as tender. When I look at them I see my past, and I hope they are able to see in me something of their future.

I have looked out these classroom windows for twenty-four years. Through these stories I hope to allow the reader to look in.

1. The Story of Two Quilts

Now that my five-year-old niece, Maren, has entered kindergarten, we have an on-going philosophical discussion about education. "Teachers know everything!" she says, often and adamantly. "Since you are a teacher, you know everything!"

"No," I say. "Teachers know some things. Nobody knows everything."

"Yes," she says stubbornly, "Teachers know everything."

"But there are some things you know that your teacher doesn't know."

"Like what?"

"Like what it feels like to be Molly's big sister, to be your Mommy and Daddy's older daughter, to be Gary's good friend, to be my five-year-old niece."

But so far she hasn't bought it. She insists teachers know everything.

In my twenty-five years of teaching middle school, one of my goals has been for my classroom to be a blend of some of the things I know, and some of the things my students know.

The quilt experiences serve as an example. Two years ago, while I was teaching at Dolores Middle School, I read in the daily bulletin that an anonymous donor was offering up to $200 to teachers of academic classes for art projects relating to

1

their curriculum. I began thinking about how I could use art to further enhance our studies of women in my sixth grade core class.

We were well into the semester, and had already written extensive autobiographies, written essays for a contest sponsored by the National Association of Women, and researched African American men and women's lives for Black History Month. My idea was to have the students feel connected not only to the lives of women in science, politics, art, social reform, music, sports, literature, journalism, space, law, civil rights, education, humor, etc., but also to the women in their own families.

I wrote a proposal to the administration explaining my idea for the quilt project and soon after was granted the money. We began class discussions on how to proceed. I put a big piece of butcher paper on the blackboard, with the word Inclusive at the top, and asked the students to develop a list of what we needed to keep in mind in order to make our quilt truly inclusive. Hands popped up, and students volunteered categories first. We should have women in medicine. Sports. Law. Civil rights. The list grew.

What else? How else can we make this quilt inclusive? What else do we know about diversity? Hands popped up again to create a second list. We should have Native American women. Hispanic American women. European American women. African American women. Asian American women. Lesbian women. Straight women. Again, our list grew. Then, we put the two lists aside, taped to the wall, so we could still see them. We began to brainstorm a third list of individual women who were possibilities for quilt squares. Before beginning to choose which woman to honor on our square, we created a very long list of possibilities. This list included people like Nancy Reagan, Jackie Kennedy, and Martha Washington, who did not end up on the final quilt itself, because the students decided that they didn't want to have a lot of presidents' wives on the quilt. They ended up honoring Eleanor Roosevelt and Abigail Adams, who fit other categories on the first list, such as social reform.

When we finished brainstorming our third list, we noticed that we didn't have anyone who was a Filipina American, and there is a large Filipino community in our school. We sent two students downstairs to the Filipino Bilingual class to explain our project, and to ask them for suggestions on Filipina women we could honor on our quilt. These students returned to class and told us the story of Vicky Draves. We learned that she was the first American woman to win the gold medal in the diving category at the Olympics. She still lives in San Francisco in the South of Market neighborhood, and the Filipino community is lobbying to get a city gymnasium named in her honor. She used to practice diving as a child by pulling her sister's mattress from the bottom bunk onto the floor, and diving off the top bunk. (Students were of course warned not to try this, as they might end up in the hospital instead of the Olympics.)

Melissa and Mariko decided they wanted to work together on her patch. Other students knew immediately whom they wanted to honor. Some had a hard time choosing between several possibilities. When they discussed this with me individually, we would look at our first two lists, and consider which choice would make our quilt most inclusive. By this time in the semester, the class was committed to including women of color as a high priority.

But Alicia wandered around for two or three days, looking at reference books, and becoming gloomier and gloomier.

"What is it, Alicia?"

"I can't find anybody that I want to do. When I think of someone, somebody else has already got her. I don't like this assignment. I don't want to do it."

"Who are the women in your life that you really care about?"

Pause. "Damara Bennett. My ballet teacher."

'Well, why don't you do a patch honoring your ballet teacher?"

She immediately brightens up. "Can I do that?"

"Yes, you can do that. You won't be able to read any books or articles on her, but you can do primary research through interviews, phone calls, or letters. That shouldn't be a problem for you, since I know you go to ballet lessons every day, and see her frequently."

Alicia's whole attitude towards this assignment changes. The next day she brings in her pink toe shoes to use as models as she fabric-paints her square. The other students admire the shoes, and she gets to talk about her dancing. My other ballerina student decides to do a patch on Isadora Duncan.

Before we begin the quilt, the students bring up the question of grading and evaluation. I have told them that I envision the quilt to be a work of art that will inspire and teach other people about the lives of women in America. I see the quilt hanging in the classroom, in other schools, in libraries, post offices, in other public places, and I see it accompanied by a book, with the women listed in alphabetical order, and with a statement by each artist telling who that woman is, and why he/she chose to honor her on this quilt. So the assignment has two parts: the quilt square, and the written piece for the book.

This causes great concern. "But some of us have never sewn anything before, and some people might be really great sewers. It's not fair to grade us on our first attempt at something."

"True. I want you to feel comfortable taking some artistic risks here. So, what shall we do?"

"Well, we're already really good writers, but we don't know yet if we're any good at sewing. Maybe we should just be graded on the written part." (I take a moment to silently do a little dance with myself because they are identifying themselves as "really good writers," which they would not have done at the beginning of the year.)

"That isn't fair to the ones who are better artists than writers," other students protest. After some discussion, we decide that they will all do the best work that they can on both the quilt square and the written piece, and they can each choose later which part they would prefer to be graded on. This feels fair to everyone.

We spend a few days doing research in the library and in the classroom. We talk about how to use symbols to represent a person's values and accomplishments. Meanwhile, I telephone my friend Ellen in Santa Cruz, who is a fifth grade teacher and an art teacher. My art skills are limited, to say the least. She suggests that I buy some black fabric to frame each square and to frame the quilt itself. "It will kind of tie things together," she tells me.

I go to the store and buy lots of unbleached muslin for the squares, some black cotton fabric for the borders, and a large variety of solid and patterned bits of colorful material. I also purchase lots of embroidery thread, needles, and embroidery hoops.

I take the whole class on a field trip, walking four blocks to the Names Project headquarters. The Names Project collects 4 by 6 foot quilt squares made by the family and friends of people who have died of AIDS. The class has just finished our nine-week family life unit, and this is the last trip we are taking to see how our community is responding to the AIDS crisis. Nancy Katz, the education director at the headquarters, meets us outside. She greets us and asks the students to come inside, past the sewing machines and the people working on them, and to sit on the floor in a circle. She tells us about her job; she explains the history and the meaning of the Names Project. She shows us the shelves and shelves of folded quilt squares. She plays us a video about the Names Quilt in Washington. After answering student questions, she gives us a poster for our classroom, and since the artist of the poster is in the room, he comes and signs it for us. We look at the quilt squares hanging on display, the symbols on them, the love and care stitched into them. They are inspiring. We tell Nancy about our incipient quilt project, and she is very supportive and enthusiastic. "I will come and help you put it together," she tells us, "and I will loan you some tools that will make measuring and cutting easier." I thank her.

As we are walking back home, red-headed Deirdre starts walking next to me and measures her steps to mine. I know she has something to say and I wait for it to come. "Can I do her?" she asks, meaning Nancy. "Yes, what a good idea," I reply. "I will give you her phone number, and you can arrange for a time to interview her. I think she would be happy to be on our quilt."

Roberta, Deirdre's best friend, says, "Can I do Deirdre's mother? She's the woman I admire most in the world."

Yes, I say. I believe in saying yes to my students. Sometimes I say no, but I don't say it lightly, and I try to give all my reasons. I believe that students have reasons behind their requests, and that it is important for me to learn about them in order to really teach effectively. Usually by the time I have to say no to a student's request, I have built up a fair amount of trust because of all my yeses.

"Can Juan and I work together? We both want to do Julie Croteau, the first woman to ever play on a college male baseball team, and we're not good at sewing, so can we work together?"

Yes.

"Can I do Dian Fossey? Annie already signed up for her, but I REALLY wanted to do her, she's the only person I REALLY want to do. No, I don't want to work WITH Annie, we don't work well together. Can I?"

Yes. It is revealing to compare these two Dian Fosseys later. The male artist has a big gorilla overpowering the square and no Dian. The female artist has put Dian in the center of the square, with a small gorilla in the background.

"Ms. Logan, can I take my square home and work on it?" Yes. "Can my mother help me?" Yes. "Ms. Logan, I have made two squares on Isadora Duncan and I don't know which one I like best."

"They're both wonderful. Let's put them both on. After all, this is a quilt about being inclusive."

Seventh and eighth graders, who are not officially part of this sixth-grade core assignment, begin to hear about the quilt and volunteer to join us. They come in at lunch time. "Can we do a patch too?" Yes. "I have some great fabric at home that I want to use. Can I bring it in?" Yes. "Can I do Cyndi Lauper?" Yes. "Can I sew on buttons, ribbons, sparkles?" Yes. "Can I stuff cotton underneath to make it three dimensional?" Yes. "Can I do Shakespeare's Juliet, even though she's not a real woman?" Yes. "The only thing I really care about is swimming. Can I do someone in swimming?" Yes. (Hence, Esther Williams.) "I want to represent all the women who were here before Columbus 'discovered' this land. Can I do the Forgotten Woman?" YES!

"Ms. Logan," Julie asks, "Can I do you?" Yes, I would be honored. "I already figured out what I'm going to do—I'm going to put your necklaces on my patch."

Frankie, an eighth grader, asks if she can do herself as Future Woman. What a good idea, I reply, and give her a blank patch.

The next day, she brings in the completed square, along with a poem for the book:

> Faces
> From the past
> Fade
> Exist only
> In memory
> Faces
> From the present
> Are in the moment
> But only for the moment
> But
> Faces
> Of the future
> Are forever
> Because future
> is infinite
> So many possibilites

Frankie is a professional actress. She wins city-wide visual arts contests and awards in the annual NOW essay contest. She sings with the school choir. She excels in math and science. To say she is a student with many possibilities is to understate.

I bring my sewing machine, my iron and my ironing board to class. I buy a set of lower- and upper-case letter stamps and a black ink pad. We decide to put each woman's name at the bottom of her patch, to add continuity to the quilt. We begin to set up stations in the room—this desk for stamping your patch, this area for measuring and cutting, this area for ironing, this area to learn embroidery stitches, this area for fabric paints. Students who are experts in each thing sit next to that area to help others.

One of the first things I notice is that only girls gravitate towards the ironing board, and only boys gravitate towards the measuring and cutting area. Every other station has both boys and girls working together. I think about what to do about this. Finally, I decide to ask Frank, a male colleague and friend, to drop by class and to casually start to help us by ironing. I am hoping that he will inspire the boys to try it. The next day, Frank does just this. He comes in, admires all the activity, and asks the girls if he can help by ironing for a while. I help with the measuring and cutting. Immediately, several boys gravitate to the ironing board and ask my friend if they can help. While they are ironing, I go over and visit.

"Do you iron at home?" I ask them. "Oh, yes, I do all the ironing at home," one of them says. "I do napkins and tee shirts," another one reports. They all iron at home.

"You're very good at it," I tell them. It wasn't that they couldn't do it. It wasn't even that they didn't want to do it, since they were certainly eager enough to help once Frank was in charge. They just needed a man there to give them support to do a "girl's job" in the public arena of the classroom.

I give some thought as to who I want to honor on my patch. I decide to honor Brenda Flyswithhawks, who is also named Eagle Woman. She is a member of the Bird Clan of the Cherokee Nation. She is a medicine woman, the first woman in her clan to get a Ph.D., and a teacher of psychology at Santa Rosa Junior College. She is a friend and a mentor. I have heard her speak several times, and I remember her saying that to be an educated Indian woman is like having a foot in each of two canoes, in rapid waters, always balancing two cultures. I decide to put two canoes and rapid water on her patch, with an eagle's wing by one canoe, and her doctoral degree by the other canoe. I read that the Cherokee Nation believes that the people came from the stars, from the Seven Pleiades, so I buy seven glass stars to sew in the corner, and, because I myself love the moon, I buy a glass moon to put on as well.

I am having a good time cutting out my canoes, stitching them onto my patch, stamping Brenda's name at the bottom of the square, painting the eagle's wing, and writing my piece for the book. Several computers have been set around the room so that students can type their written pieces onto discs when they are ready.

A parent brings in some of her own fabric paints and a book of designs that can be ironed on fabric for embroidery outlines. She stays to show us how to use the materials.

As the patches are finished, we use masking tape to fix them to the blackboard, making new rows when needed. We discuss how many rows to have, how many patches to a row.

John is having a hard time with Georgia O'Keefe. He has a good image in his mind, but he can't get it to work on the square. I send him to work with Suzanne, our AV clerk, who I know is a good artist, and a kind and patient person. She herself has volunteered to do a patch on Joan Baez.

A young woman who works as a part-time aide in the special education department, and who studies art part time, takes home a blank muslin square. She returns it with an incredibly realistic air-brushed portrait of Billy Holliday.

One sixth grader, Thomas, has been struggling with cancer since he was six months old. He has undergone radiation treatment, chemotherapy, and surgery, and he has lost an eye. This is the first time he has stayed a whole year in school since third grade. Writing his autobiography was very traumatic for him; it involved building a lot of trust in class and helping Thomas to realize that he too had had a "real life." In the end he was able to claim his illness as a part of his life and even included pictures of himself in the hospital, bald and frail after chemotherapy. Thomas chooses to dedicate his quilt square to a family friend and film maker, Felicia Lowe. In his written entry, he tells about Felicia's first film, "China, Land of My Father." Then Thomas writes, "Two years later her second child was born. She wanted to make another film but when they discovered that her daughter had leukemia, she could not continue. It took two years for the chemotherapy to destroy the dangerous form of cancer. When her daughter was well, Felicia went to Angel Island to make her second film." Thomas goes on to provide more information about Felicia's film career, but it is the caretaking of her daughter that is the real story here. In telling it, Thomas has stitched his own story onto our quilt.

As each square is completed, we use masking tape to fix it to the blackboard. The class responds positively each time. The exceptionally beautiful ones make the whole quilt look better. The less-than-beautiful ones look nicer among the others. Nobody says, "Mine is better than yours." We are each a part of a whole.

It is time to measure and cut the black fabric and to sew the rows of patches together. Not everyone is finished with his or her patch, but we begin with the rows that are complete. We are doing fine until my sewing machine breaks. I call parents for help. The next day, Linda Clayton and Carol Larson arrive with their portable sewing machines. They stay for several days. They sew while students iron open seams, work on the computers, or help others. I take time out now and then to notice and appreciate what is going on. The energy in the room is calm and relaxed, but focused and productive. Students are self-directed and supportive of one another.

Jesse is working on a patch about his grandmother, who took him and his Dad to New Zealand over the Christmas break to visit her birthplace, a sheep farm. Jesse decides to put a sheep, a kiwi, the airplane they took to New Zealand, and a rose (which is his grandmother's birthday month flower) onto his square. He also decides to learn how to embroider the entire patch since his grandmother loves to embroider. It is the first time he has used needle and thread, and he does a remarkably good job. Jesse is a great outgoing kid, but he is sometimes disruptive and not always cooperative. When we rode a streetcar to an ice skating field trip, Jesse got in trouble for riding on the back of the trolley, through the tunnel no less . To watch him quietly absorbed in his embroidery is a special thrill.

Shoshannah lost her great-grandmother, Bubby, in February. She writes about this loss for her quilt piece, and for her square she decides to embroider her family tree, with Bubby as the trunk. Her mother, her aunts and uncles, her cousins, her brother and herself are all branches and twigs, and she embroiders their family names. But most of her time is spent painstakingly stitching different shades of brown into the thick, strong trunk. She sews her grief and her love for her great-grandmother into her patch. She works on it in class and at home, but it is the last to be added to the rows on the blackboard, and at that she still doesn't have enough time to finish. She ends up having to color in the small unstitched part of the trunk with brown fabric paint.

The student I have been most worried about chooses Esther Williams as the subject of her square. This child's own story unfolded slowly this year, and it took many hours of counseling and support services from social workers to get her out of an abusive home. Her patch shows Esther Williams in a typical synchronized swimming pose — head pointing toward the bottom of the pool, legs pointing out of the water toward the sky — but I notice that the swimmer has no arms. This could be because it is difficult to depict the sculling action necessary to hold this position. It could also be her artistic rendition of her emotional state. I also notice a colorful, happy mermaid perched on the edge of a wave, looking over this upside-down swimmer.

Another student, who has had troubles this year, has decided to do Dorothy from *The Wizard of Oz*. But, early in the project she comes to me and asks, "Can I do my witchery teacher, Starhawk, instead?" "Yes," I reply. It seems Starhawk has done some healing work with her this year. I give the student one of my glass stars to sew onto her patch, rationalizing that we can usually only see six of the seven Pleides, anyway.

Alberto carefully embroiders four images of women in a square honoring all Mothers. Garrett, whose writing always contains many references to blood and gore, does a generic quilt square dedicated to women doctors. But the doctor he depicts wears a blood-splattered white gown and holds a huge needle dripping blood in one hand and a bloody scalpel in the other. On the examining table huddles a small, scared child, who looks a lot like Garrett.

Our personal histories and our class experiences are stitched together. The eighth grade student we have seen through a suicide attempt sews a square honoring Cyndi Lauper, and writes about how much Cyndi's music has helped her. Her best friend, Rebecca, does her patch on Juliet, the only heroine from literature on our quilt, and also a thirteen-year-old who kills herself.

Another eighth-grade student wanted to do her square on Anne of Green Gables. She even talked one of her red-headed friends into cutting several inches of her hair so that she can give Anne real braids. But, unfortunately, she doesn't get around to sewing a patch. The idea stays just an idea, and her friend's hair is shorter for nothing.

It is now June, just a few days before the end of the term. Each step we take transforms the quilt. Our squares are framed in black, and we have a border. Carol takes the quilt home and spends an evening stitching in the cotton batting and sewing on the backing sheet. The next day we spread the quilt out on several tables and take turns knotting through the front, batting, and backing. Meanwhile, we finish typing up our pieces into the computer.

I bring the discs to my friend, Craig Johnson, who donates his time to print them professionally. I run off copies for each student and make a special copy that will hang next to the quilt. The day before the end of the term, we take the quilt outside to photograph it. During lunch, I take the film to be processed and order enough copies so that each student will have a photo of the entire quilt and a close-up of his or her own patch, as well as a copy of our quilt book.

I buy two copies of *Hearts and Hands*, a book about women and quilts, to give to Linda and Carol, the parents who helped us. I pass the books around the room so the students can write their own personal thank-yous on the blank pages at the front and back of the book. "Without you," one boy writes, "our quilt would just be scraps of fabric."

Someone says, "Don't you wish we could each take it home and sleep under it, and write down our dreams?"

The finished quilt is colorful and diverse. No two patches are the same. I have provided the outline, the framework for the assignment, but each participant has created something uniquely their own.

Why did this assignment work? I ask myself. I think about my favorite frameworks for teaching. The Bay Area Writing Project is an organization of successful teachers of writing who work together to improve the teaching of writing in schools.

They have identified the five phases of writing. Prewriting is everything that is done before putting pencil to paper—listing, thinking, researching, discussing, drawing. *Writing for fluency* is writing for content only, letting one's thoughts flow onto paper without worrying about spelling or grammatical correctness. *Response* is reviewing one's writing and revising for content—adding, deleting, explaining, clarifying. *Writing for form* involves checking spelling, neatness, grammar, punctuation, in preparation for *publication and/or evaluation.* Yes, we followed the whole process in writing the quillt the book. We stressed process more than product, and we stayed with that process until we had produced good writing.

I think once again about the relation my work has to Peggy McIntosh's theory of Interactive Phases of Curricular Re-vision. It has both illuminated and informed my work. Peggy, who is associate director of The Center for Research on Women at Wellesley College and the founder of S.E.E.D. (Seeking Educational Equity and Diversity), describes various phases one can go through when attempting to include under-represented people in curriculum. I am grateful to have discovered such a clear, succinct description of the varieties of inclusiveness, as well as an inspiring mentor. Since first reading her work, I have often had a large piece of paper taped to the chalkboard in my classroom with the heading, "Judy Logan's Oversimplification of Peggy McIntosh's Interactive Phases of Curriculum."

Here is a brief synopsis of her theory: In Phase One: There are no women or people of color in the curriculum and nobody notices that they are missing. In Phase Two people begin to notice how many are missing, so they look around for exceptional Others who act enough like famous white men to be put into history. This phase stresses role models and heroes, but they are presented as unlike their kind. Phase Three: Historians *want* to put a lot of women and people of color into history, but they can't find any except protesters who focus on issues of conflict—sexism, racism, classism—and who are aware of systemic hierarchies and oppression. Everyone seems angry. In Phase Four, history, or curriculum, is *refocused* to put everyday life at the center. Now remarkable people don't have to behave in a certain way (i.e., like famous men) to get into history; everything they do *is* history. Phase One through Three describe aspects of our psyches and our society that show our capacities to make and sustain pecking orders. Phase Four describes our ability to make and sustain relationships and to live non-violently in a diverse habitat. Phase Five will put the elements of phases One, Two, Three (creating pecking orders) into better balance with Phase Four (living in symbiotic relationships).

I notice that our quilt includes some Phase Two patches, like those of Abigail Adams, Elizabeth Blackwell, Amelia Earhart, Sojourner Truth, Harriet Tubman, and Alice Walker. Some may be thought of as Phase Three patches, such as the ones for Ida B. Wells, a journalist who protested lynching, or Ann Simonton, who said women were not just "pieces of meat" and dressed herself in raw steaks in Santa Cruz to protest the beauty pageants held there. There is also Lolita Lebron, the Puerto Rican woman who spent many years in jail for bursting into Congress shooting and shouting for Puerto Rican inde-pendence, and finally, Forgotten Woman, representing the many Native American women left out of history books. And we have many Phase Four patches, like Nancy Katz, Deidre's mother, Jesse's grandmother, Alicia's ballet teacher, the class-room teacher (me), generic patches for mothers, doctors, and astronauts, and my personal favorite, Future Woman. We even have a Phase One womanless patch: the one in which Dian Fossey is represented by a large gorilla. I feel that this balance of phases makes ours a Phase Five quilt.

I think, too, about Anthony F. Gregoric's description of learning styles. He tells us that students can be divided into four major categories of learning: concrete/sequential, random/concrete, abstract/sequential, and random/abstract. Learners are dominant either in the abstract world (writing, philosophizing) or the concrete world (building houses, sewing clothes). There has been a place in this quilt assignment for those who function best in each of these worlds. Some students organize their learning sequentially, one step at a time in an orderly fashion. Some students work randomly, jumping to and focusing on areas of significance for them, and filling in the gaps later. This assignment has provided for these differences as well.

I note that in working on our quilt project we have used the educational philosopher Benjamin Bloom's categories of cognitive skills. Bloom categorized learning as knowledge, or the ability to learn facts and information; comprehension, or the ability to understand facts and information; application, the ability to apply learned knowledge to new tasks; synthesis, the ability to combine information and understand relationships of learned material; and evaluation, the ability to judge the relevance and importance of information. I have observed a lot of creativity, and we have developed skills such as listening, cooperating, teaching, sharing, and encouraging. The process of making the quilt has brought us closer together as a class. Even those of us who sewed less than perfect patches delight in the finished product.

I think about my own guidelines on inclusive curriculum. As much as possible, if I control the content, I try to let students control the form. If I control the form, I try to let students control the content. I think of this as the "have tos" and the "get tos," as in yes, you "have to" do a quilt patch. Yes, you "have to" do a woman, BUT you "get to" choose the woman you want to honor on this quilt, and you "get to" do your patch any way you want to.

I ask myself, did this lesson empower my students, or was it an instance of the teacher telling them what to do and how to do it.

Was the project a doubting game? Did we begin by doubting everything until it has been defended and proved? Did we learn through skepticism, and attack new ideas? Or was the process a believing game, through which we began by accepting, walking in the other's shoes, postponing disbelief, and learning by identifying?

Was it about care and connection, or was it about winning and losing?

Did it get across the idea that history is all of us?

Emily Style is a teacher and, with Peggy McIntosh, co-directs the National Seeking Educational Equity and Diversity (S.E.E.D.) Project on inclusive curricula. The project prepares K-12 teachers to lead school-based, year-long reading groups with other teachers to discuss making school curricula gender-fair and multicultural. Her educational philosophy is expressed through the metaphor of windows and mirrors. She believes that all students should be able to see themselves mirrored in the content of curriculum, in terms of gender, ethnicity, race, and class. At the same time students should also be able to look through the windows of curriculum into the stories of people who are "other" to them. This quilt as a collection of windows and mirrors. In their small black frames, some patches are windows, others mirrors, some both. We see ourselves reflected in this quilt.

The quilt travels with me when I do summer workshops in Colorado, Minnesota, New Jersey and California. Other teachers respond to it favorably. Peggy McIntosh says she likes quilts because, among other things, "there is no head patch." This is true; it has felt like a non-hierarchical assignment. When we taped the patches to the blackboard, they fit without any preconceived ordering. Nobody fought about whose patch was first, or last.

A good curriculum is like a poem that follows a particular pattern, but that allows the audience to bring their own experiences to the construction of meaning. It leaves a corner open for the reader to enter. Not only did each student bring her or his own experiences into the quilt (Shoshannah's family tree, Frankie's vision of herself in the future, Garrett's bloody doctor), but each observer of the quilt is encouraged to participate. (What woman would you choose to put on your patch? Who is missing from this quilt? Who on this quilt do you already know? Who is a stranger to you?) I think all curriculum should be like this. Yes, there needs to be a form, an outline, clear expectations, but there also needs to be that corner open for the students' stories to enter in.

My friend Sara takes our quilt to Esprit, a well-known clothing manufacturer in San Francisco that collects and displays quilts, and their professional photographer takes better pictures of it, and gives me the negatives. After a short display in the glass case of the school library, the quilt hangs in my classroom.

The next year, when the new sixth grade class comes into my room and sees the quilt, they say, "Will we get to do a quilt too?"

Oh yes, I say, wondering whether I will have the time and energy for it at the end of the term, wondering where I will get the money. But a parent of a former student has received a grant to do art in the schools. He volunteers to teach the quilt unit. *He* will buy and pay for the fabric. *He* will plan the borders. *He* will sew the batting and the backing together, and supervise the work in class. I can be one of the students, just making my own patch, writing my own piece. I am very grateful. I don't have to spend my own money or spend my lunch periods at the fabric store, and I don't have to use my math skills to figure out how many inches each patch will be, or how many patches to a row. Thus begins the story of the second quilt.

Alan, the parent in charge of this assignment, and I work out our time schedules. I have the students two periods in a row, so he decides to come in two days a week, and work for a two- hour stretch. That way we won't spend a lot of time putting materials out, and then putting them away again. The iron and the ironing board return to school. The students and I work on how to choose a person to honor on the quilt, how to do research on that person's life, and how to write a piece for the book that will hang next to the quilt.

Hanako, who was so very seriously ill this year that she required hospitalization and many painful blood transfusions, decides to do a square on Gilda Radner, the Saturday Night Live comedienne who died of cervical cancer. Leslie chooses Lucille Ball, who has also just died.

Emma does a patch on "Teacher Love," her nickname for her pre-school teacher, Sylvia Bradley.

Ethan does his patch on Jane Goodall; Janet chooses Zora Neale Hurston. Johannes picks Helen Keller; Tabashi, Annie Sullivan. Lucy chooses Louisa May Alcott, Raoul writes about Sarah Winnemucca, and Akiko does her patch on Martha Graham. Craig writes about Clara Foltz, the first woman lawyer in California. Lance does a generic quilt square on Rosie the Riveter, honoring all working class women. Christa McAuliffe, the teacher who died in the Challenger spaceship explosion, and Margaret Sanger, birth control pioneer, are also included. This year, the idea that history is all of us has really sunk in, and eighteen of the thirty-five squares honor the students' mothers, grandmothers, aunts or godmothers.

The riveting square that looks like Lana Turner, with her blonde hair pulled over one eye, is really Molly's story about her relative Lana Smith, who was a pioneer farmhand and who lost her eye after it was hit by a rock.

Matt writes about his great-grandmother. Andy, Gabriela, and Brian honor their grandmothers; Stella, Susan, Ralph, Samantha, Julia, Robbie, Melanie and Jason choose to do their mothers. Rose writes about her mother's best friend, Louise Jones, Rose's "godmother and heroine," who is a composer. One day, Rose's mother stops by school, and I bring her up to my room to see the quilt in progress. We both stand there admiring it. She gets teary and says how wonderful it is to see her best friend included. She tells me the story of one of Louise's compositions called "Emily's Nap." Louise had adopted a young daughter, Emily, who was hyperactive and who never slept during the day. This composition was for the drums, and was a noisy rendition of the reality of Emily's non-existent "naptime."

When students finish their writing for the book, I sign them into the computer lab for the final printing.

The process of quilt-making is different this time. Alan cuts out all of the squares for us. He talks to us about the skills he will teach us — how to draw portraits so that the eyes are in the middle of the egg-shaped face, how to cut out rubber stamps backwards so that the letters appear correctly on the patch, how to mix fabric paints to get proper flesh tones, how to paint backgrounds in colors that enhance your portrait, how to frame your square in contrasting colors to deepen the effect. He talks to us about symbols, and he shows us the square of his grandmother that he has painted as an example.

Each of us brings in a photograph of the woman we are portraying for the quilt. We consult them carefully as we make our preliminary drawings. I've chosen Faye Wattleton, the president of Planned Parenthood, and I use the photograph of her with her daughter from the book of photographs *I Dream A World*. Alan does a stunning second square on Ella Fitzgerald.

We begin our drawings on tracing paper, then trace the outlines of our drawing in black felt pens, then tape our muslin squares over the black outlined drawings on the windows, so that the dark lines show through. When we have traced the basic shapes onto the fabric, we are ready to go to the art room to begin mixing the paints for the skin tones. We use each others' skin for examples, and I love watching my class ask their Asian American, European American, or African American classmates to put their forearms near their patch while they struggle to mix the exact shade. Jason agrees to be my model for Faye Wattleton's skin.

Alan is incredibly well-organized, patient, knowledgeable, and talented. He has a vision of how this quilt will look, and what skills he wants to teach us, and I notice a subtle thing happening. The students begin to ask questions. "I'm painting my grandmother, and I would like to bring in some of her earrings to sew on the quilt."

No, but you may paint the earrings on.

"Can I bring in some special buttons to put on her dress?"

No, but you may paint the buttons on.

"Can I do a profile of my person?"

No, in the interests of continuity, all of our portraits will be full face.

"Can I stuff cotton in mine to make it puff out?"

No.

In order to make his vision (and it is a lovely one) work, Alan needs to say no to the students' visions. There are a lot of "have tos," and not enough "get tos."

Something happens to students when we say no to them. There is a subtle but real disconnection. A resignation. A giving up. Sometimes, resentment. I watch it happen.

The resulting quilt is dazzling. It doesn't sag or gap like our first year quilt. Instead of having black borders, each square is framed in a contrasting color. Students have painted in the entire square, so the overall effect is richer. But when I look at each individual square and begin to talk about the stories behind each patch, I often can't remember which child did which square. They look too much alike. I worry about what might have been sacrificed in order to make this vision work.

Again, I photograph the quilt and order forty copies. I photograph each square so each child will go home with a picture of the quilt, a close-up picture of his or her square, and a copy of the quilt book. I plan an evening to display the quilt, give out the pictures, and say good-bye, since I am leaving for a one-year sabbatical. We invite all of the parents, as well as the aunts, grandmothers, godmothers, teachers, and mothers who are honored on the quilt. I bring two cakes that say Congratulations Seventh Graders, since they have all just passed into the next grade. The students also bring cakes and cookies. We move the tables aside, set out chairs in rows for our guests, put out coffee, tea, napkins, and paper plates.

The completed quilt hangs at the front of the room. Alan has even bought a bamboo pole from which to hang it. Each student takes a turn coming to the front of the room, pointing out his or her patch, and telling the story of the person he or she is honoring. It is a treat for me to watch this affect the audience. Aunts smile, grandmothers get teary, everybody feels good. Only one mother feels that her daughter chose to do her because "she was too lazy to do research on anyone else."

When the two quilts hang side by side, they are each beautiful. The second quilt shows that each student went through the process of learning portraiture techniques and has learned something about color theory and mixing and using fabric paints. Each square is a face. By controlling both the form and the content of the lesson (what we are doing and how we are doing it), there has been less room for experimentation on the part of the students. Their own stories have not surfaced.

So the first one is still my favorite. When my five-year-old niece is old enough to understand, I'll use it as an example to further explain to her that teachers don't know everything. Students have their own stories.

2. Stealing Stories

A few days after I had attended a theater performance with a large group of seventh and eighth graders, a parent telephoned. "Judy," she said, "this phone call is strictly confidential. Please don't let on that I've called you, but something has happened that I think you should know about."

She proceeds to tell me that her daughter and three of her good friends, each of whom was an excellent, well-behaved student, had gone to Woolworth's five-and-ten-cent store on the way home from the theater, and were caught stealing something—I think it was a lipstick. All four of them were brought to the manager's office, lectured, threatened with the police, and kept there until their parents could come and pick them up. The girl's mother then tells me that her daughter is really remorseful and ashamed, and, along with her friends, very worried that I will find out what happened and think less of them.

My Stealing Stories evolved over the years almost by accident, but have been so successful in building trust in the classroom that I now recommend them highly to other middle school teachers and parents. Basically, they are four stories about teen-agers who steal something. But the role of the wise adult figure in each story is wonderfully unusual. Instead of becoming angry, instead of shaming or humiliating the child, the adult uses the stealing incident to foster self-esteem and to develop wiser decision-making skills.

It is my experience that not all students have perfect parents. Since it is also my experience that middle school years are rife with crises, I use these stories as a way to develop a wise parent within the child, so that if a parent, or parent figure, uses a shame-based approach during a crisis, the child will have an alternative voice within.

Am I saying that the act of stealing by an adolescent is an opportunity to cultivate wisdom? Yes, I am. It is in making mistakes that we are most vulnerable, and it is in the grip of this vulnerability we are most likely to listen and grow. The flip side, of course, is that adults can do a great deal of damage during these vulnerable times. Hence the stealing stories, wherein I offer my students four adults who understand this vulnerability and who use it as an opportunity for transformation.

The first story is from the novel *Mama's Bank Account,* by Kathryn Forbes. In Chapter 11, "Mama and Big Business," Katrin is working in Schiller's Drugstore for three hours every afternoon while Mr. Schiller goes home for a hot lunch. Her friend Carmelita comes to the store to keep her company, and before long, they take to stealing a Hoeffler's Centennial candy bar every day, enjoying it, and throwing the box and wrapper up onto a shelf over the front door, to hide the evidence of their theft. They feel guilty and keep promising themselves they will stop, but they keep stealing. One day, a man comes in to change the window dressing above the store and discovers all these empty Centennial boxes, which he throws down onto the first floor. Katrin is horrified, but before she has a chance to say anything, Mrs. Schiller yells at her and lectures her, calling her a thief. Katrin rushes home to Mama in tears, and Mama offers her understanding:

"This is important, my Katrin. Perhaps I cannot explain it so well, but you must not ever feel here —" she touched me — "in your heart, that you are what you said. A—a thief A bad girl."

"But Mama, I did take them—and Mrs. Schiller said—"

"Katrin, believe me, you are not a thief. You are a good girl."
I shook my head. "You have been foolish, yes, you have done
wrong. But no great wrong. You are still so young—so greedy
for sweets, as all young things are."

"Mama, you just don't understand!"

"But I do, that is why—" And Mama's laugh rang out suddenly, richly.

Mama continues by telling Katrin about the time that she
was living with Aunt Lena, and Papa was courting her. Each
Friday night Lena would make cookies, or a cake. Once she
was able to make a beautiful cake that was piled high with
white frosting. Mama was young and she, too, had a sweet
tooth. She kept sneaking into the pantry and tasting the frosting, until finally there was no frosting left on the cake. Katrin
laughs with Mama at this story. "What happened?" she asks,
and Mama tells her that Aunt Lena served the bald cake to
Papa and told him what had happened.

"And what did Papa do?" Katrin asks. Mama smiled a secret
smile. "He married me," she said, "anyhow."

Earlier in the story, Katrin says, "But, Mama, whenever I
think of it, oh Mama, I am so ashamed."

"Is good to be ashamed," Mama replies. "That makes it
sure you will not do such a thing again. But cannot you see,
Katrin, that with the shame and the sorrow there must also be
the saving laughter?"

When I discovered how much my students loved this story,
I looked around for another one, and discovered William
Saroyan's "The Parsley Garden." This story takes place during
the depression, in Fresno, California. It is about a young boy

named Al Condraj who steals a hammer at the five-and-dime, is caught, and is made to stand in the manager's office for a long time before he is allowed to go home:

> The first thing he did when he was free was laugh, but he knew he had been humiliated and he was deeply ashamed. It was not in his nature to take things that did not belong to him. He hated the young man who had caught him and he hated the manager of the store who had made him stand in silence in the office so long. He hadn't liked it at all when the young man had said he ought to hit him over the head with the hammer. . . Of course he HAD stolen the hammer and he had been caught, but it seemed to him he oughtn't to have been so humiliated.
>
> After he had walked three blocks he decided he didn't want to go home just yet, so he turned around and started walking back to town. He almost believed he meant to go back and say something to the young man who had caught him. And then he wasn't sure he didn't mean to go back and steal the hammer again, and this time NOT get caught. As long as he had been made to feel like a thief anyway, the least he ought to get out of it was the hammer."

Al lives alone with his mother, who does seasonal work in a packing house. When he goes home he tells his mother everything that has happened.

> "I don't want you to steal," his mother said in broken English. "Here is ten cents. You go back to that man and you give him this money and you bring it home, that hammer."
>
> "No," Al Condraj said. "I won't take your money for something I don't really need."

Katrin's mother tells her a story, Al's mother offers him the price of the hammer. Each parent cherishes the child's self-esteem and trusts the humiliation of the experience itself to teach the lesson. Neither condones stealing, but neither punishes her child. On his own, Al returns to the store and gets a job shelving goods. His work is so good that the manager offers him a full-time job at a dollar a day, paying him a dollar for his first day's work. But Al takes only the hammer:

> "I left the dollar on Mr. Clemmer's desk," Al Condraj said, "and I told them both I didn't want the job."
> "Why you say that?" the woman said. "Dollar a day for eleven-year-old boy good money. Why you not take the job?"
> "Because I hate both of them," the boy said. "I would never work for people like that. I just looked at them and picked up my hammer and walked out."

Students love this story, so I offer another. "Thank you, Ma'am," by Langston Hughes, is the story of a young boy who tries to steal the purse of Mrs. Luella Bates Washington Jones. In this story, Mrs. Jones catches the young boy who tries to snatch her pocketbook, hangs on to him, and ends up bringing him home for supper. As the story progresses, we watch the boy change. Mrs. Luella Bates Washington Jones offers him her trust along with half her dinner. She discovers that the boy wants ten dollars to buy himself a pair of blue suede shoes, and she not only tells him the story of her own life, but gives him her hard-earned ten dollars before she sends him back onto the street. The boy is so overwhelmed with her kindness and generosity that he cannot get himself to say, "Thank you, Ma'am."

The next story that I read to my students, "Anita's Gift" by Carol McAfee Morgan, is about a Puerto Rican girl in New

York City who sees a bucket of roses left unattended on the sidewalk. She takes a bunch, not realizing she is stealing until she gets home. She, her mother and her grandmother are terrified that the police will arrive at any moment to arrest her. Her big brother brings her back to the place on the sidewalk and helps her return the flowers to the owner, explaining her mistake. The florist is also Puerto Rican, and he responds with kindness. He tells her that he understands her longing for flowers, since their homeland has an abundance of free and colorful flowers. He, too, misses Puerto Rico. He tells her to stop by his store every Saturday night so that he can give her some flowers to take home, as many do not last until Monday. Like the adults in the other stories, he has seen the child's need rather than the child's theft, and he has responded in such a way as to build character rather than to destroy it.

By the time we have listened to and discussed these four stories, we are ready to tell and to write stories about our own stealing experiences. I don't condone stealing. But we do talk about what we can learn from it. We also talk about how we would respond if our own children were ever caught stealing, or if they were to tell us they had stolen something. Nobody brags about stealing in these discussions, and there is an atmosphere of trust.

Sometimes I continue with two more stories—"A Lickin' A Boy Could Be Proud Of" by Helen Eustis, and "The Streets of Memphis" by Dick Gregory. The first is about a young orphan who is adopted by a childless couple who own a store. The boy is left to watch the store for a certain period every day, and, like Katrin, gives in to temptation and steals candy. It is the "lick'in" that his new dad gives him when he is caught that convinces him that the couple really love him and intend to keep him. In "The Streets of Memphis," the young boy is given a note and some money by his distraught mother who has just moved north after being abandoned by her husband. She sends her son to the store for some groceries but some neighborhood boys beat him up and steal his money. When he returns home his mother gives him another note, more money, and a big stick, and tells him he cannot come back home without the groceries. She forces him to deal with the toughness of the streets. This is a harsh story that offers many writing opportunities: Tell this story from the mother's point of view. Write a story about the same neighborhood three months later. Tell the story from a gang member's point of view. Students have strong feelings about the violence on their streets.

By now we have heard a story about a Norwegian Immigrant family, "Mama and Big Business," that takes place in San Francisco, on Castro Street, a few blocks from our school. We have heard a story about an Armenian family, "The Parsley Garden," that takes place in rural California, and we have heard the story about an encounter between an African American woman and child on the streets of Harlem, and of a Puerto Rican girl in New York.

After reading and discussing these stories, we compare and contrast our responses to those of our parents. The stories have presented us with cross-cultural themes, and in each we have found wisdom and a mirror of our own experience.

I don't know if these stories had a direct impact on the girls who stole lipstick from Woolworth's. They never talked to me about it. I did notice the glances the girls exchanged as they listened to these stories and the discussions that followed.

3. Gendered Journeys

I have spent the last thirty years knee-deep in adolescence. One phenomenon that I have observed over and over again is that as young people enter puberty they begin to identify themselves as male or female in a different and more intense way than they did as children. Their suddenly unfamiliar bodies provide undeniable evidence that they are becoming women or men. Sometimes, in order to claim this new territory and help put it in a positive light, they disparage the other sex. Boys assert that men are better than women; girls claim that women are better than men. In the classroom, such tensions translate into "sibling rivalry" on a grand scale.

In order to keep classroom teaching about gender from falling into the war of the sexes, it is important to begin by letting students focus on their own attitudes, ideas and feelings about their own and the opposite sex. Students need to realize their own habits of sexual stereotyping before they can see them at work in the world outside the classroom. Like attitudes about race and class, attitudes about gender are sometimes invisible, and we can't analyze them or begin to change them unless we make them visible.

The following lesson is one I've used to bring matters of sex and gender into focus. First, I ask students to clear their desks except for a pen or pencil and a piece of blank paper. Then, I ask them to put their heads down and close their eyes. "Today

I will be taking you on a journey back through time. This is not a real journey. It is a journey of the imagination. To begin, step out of your body and see yourself at your desk with your head down. Now, travel back through time until you are in the fifth grade. See yourself in your elementary-school classroom. What are you wearing? Who is your teacher? What are you doing? See yourself at home. What does your room look like? Who are your friends?

"Now, travel back through time until you are in the third grade. See yourself in your third grade classroom. What are you doing? What are you wearing? What do you care about? Who are your friends? What do you do after school? What does your room look like?

"Travel again to the first grade. Notice everything around you. You are learning to read. What are you reading? What does your room at home look like? What do you like to do with your free time?

"Now see yourself as a kindergartener . . . See how you are playing, who you are playing with, what you are doing. What do you love to do? What do you hate to do?

"Travel again to when you are four. Some of you may have been in a pre-school. Some of you may have been at home. Some of you may have been with a babysitter. What were you like then? Notice things around you. What toys do you play with? Now you are three . . . Look around. Now you are two . . . beginning to really talk . . . Now you are one . . . standing and moving around, learning to walk. Travel back again until you are a baby . . . Look around your room, at the people around you, at your toys. Now, travel back some more, and here you are, ready to be born! Everyone is so excited, so anxious, so happy, waiting for your birth . . . and here you are!—but this time, imagine that you are born as the opposite sex. So, if you are a boy, pretend you are born a girl. If you are a girl, pretend that you are born a boy. See yourself as a baby, coming home for the first time. Now, see yourself as a year old, learning to walk and move . . . As a two-year-old, learning to speak. . . . See yourself at the age of three. What are you wearing, what are you doing? Travel to being four, then five, entering kindergarten. See yourself playing in kindergarten. Now move to first grade . . . second grade . . . third grade . . . See yourself in fifth grade. Notice your friends, see your teacher, see yourself reading, see yourself playing after school. Look at your room at home. Now, come back to Dolores, into room 217. See yourself with your head down on your desk. Come back into your body, and when you are ready, open your eyes and sit up. Without talking to anybody, please write a list of how your life seems different since you have been born as a person of the other sex. No one will see this list but you, so be honest."

My students are always very quiet and intense during this list writing. While they are writing their lists, I tape two large pieces of butcher paper onto my blackboard, labeling one "MALES," the other "FEMALES." When students have finished their lists, I say, "Now I would like to go around the room and have each of you choose one thing from your list to share with the class. If this feels difficult, you have the right to pass. Before we start with this side of the room, I would like to add just one more rule. Girls, the boys might say something about being female that doesn't feel true to us. That's okay, we'll have a chance to tell them how it really is to be female later. Right now, it's important just to listen *so we can begin to understand what they think being female is all about.* And boys, the same is true for you. You may hear us saying things about being male that don't feel true to you. Again, you'll have a chance to set us straight later.

For now, *listen carefully, so you can begin to understand what our concepts of being male are.*" This is an important caution. Without it, this exercise can deteriorate into a verbal battle between the sexes.

As students volunteer statements from their lists, I write them under the "MALE" list if the students are male, under "FEMALE" if they are female. The boys generally see their female lives in terms of things they would "have to" do, and activities they wouldn't "get to" do. The statements the boys volunteer include: I'd have to talk on the phone a lot, I'd have to have a pink bedroom, I'd worry about getting pregnant, I'd have to get up earlier in the morning so I'd have time to fix my hair and look nice, I wouldn't get to play football, I'd have to giggle a lot, I'd have to do the dishes, I'd have to spend a lot of time in the bathroom.

Girls, however, generally see masculine pursuits as things they *would* "get to" do, with a few "have to's" thrown in. They say things like, I'd have to be tough, I could sleep later in the morning because I wouldn't care how I looked, I could play more sports, I could stay out later, I wouldn't have to babysit.

Perceptive Ellie grumbles, "I think this is a sexist assignment! There are no differences between the sexes. Pass." (You may be right, I tell her later, but lots of people *think* there are differences, and it's important for us to find out what they think.)

Once we have gone around the room, I give students the opportunity to raise their hands and add things from their private lists that they would like to see on our butcher paper list. Usually a third to a half of the class adds more items. When a student adds something that is already on the list, I star it. Sometimes an item like the pink bedroom statement gets two or three stars.

When our lists are complete, I go over the statements again, only this time students have an opportunity to respond to the lists made about their sex. So, if Johnny has said he would "have to" have a pink bedroom if he were female, I would say, "Johnny, what color bedroom do you have now?"

"White."

I give him a big smile. "My bedroom is white too!!! Girls, how many of you have a white bedroom?" Several hands go up. "Girls, how many of you do *not* have a pink bedroom?" Most hands go up. "So, Johnny, the good news is that if you were female, you wouldn't have to have a pink bedroom.."

The tone is important here, because we have all received many messages from our popular culture about stereotyping and grievance in the gender arena, as evidenced by these very lists my students have produced. One only need watch television an hour or two, listen to music popular with teenagers, or read newspapers for a short time to see what these vulnerable youngsters are exposed to and how erroneous these messages can be. Too many adolescents are not offered dignified examples of what it is to be male or female in our world. To keep this exercise from being about winning and losing, ("boys are better" or "girls are better"), I try to present it as an exploration of our hidden assumptions, careful detective work aimed at cracking the code of what it means to be male or female. The exercise should not be about making anybody feel bad, even if what they say might seem outrageous.

When we have finished going over the lists a second time, checking them against our own experiences, I pass out an article published in Redbook Magazine called, "How Would Your Life Be Different?" We read it aloud together. This article describes the results of a similar exercise done with sixth grade children in Colorado. These students said extreme things: "If I were born a girl I'd kill myself," and "If I were born a boy, maybe my Daddy would like me." My students are shocked by what these children are saying. They immediately try to distance themselves from them.

"Oh, well, that was in Colorado. Everyone knows that people in California aren't like that. Especially in San Francisco."

Oh? Let's take a look at our own lists, tacked up in the front of our room. Our own lists reflect the same stereotypes along the lines of appearance, behavior, etc. Because we began this lesson with our own experiences, students are less able to dismiss the information presented in the Redbook article. They can begin to own the problem—that our culture projects clear expectations onto people of either sex. While there are advantages and disadvantages connected with each projected image, the advantages are clearly perceived to be primarily for males, the disadvantages primarily for females. The students then participate in class activities on gender more fully. They don't have to be in the "girl camp" or the "boy camp." They shift from the personal view to an awareness that as females certain pressures and expectations are exerted on them that may or may not fit who they really are. The same is true for boys. Many boys don't play sports. Many girls don't have pink bedrooms with doll collections. I notice also that the class receives information on gender differently, with a more skeptical attitude, and begin to perceive that their own gender-filter affects their thinking, feelings, and attitudes.

This kind of self-examination is essential to critical thinking, not only within classrooms addressing gender issues like mine, but in the home. Gender work is not just about including women in curriculum, although that is an essential part of it. It is about bringing a critical self-awareness into every corner of our lives.

4. Random Accounts of Connected Knowing

I have planned a Significant Lesson. As I begin to present this lesson, I notice that all of the students are properly attending to what I have to say, with the exception of four girls at one back table who are quietly absorbed in doing something else. I grow annoyed. Here I am being Significant in a well-prepared way, and these four are not captivated.

I move closer to their table, hoping that my proximity will encourage better attention. I notice that they have taken crayons and felt markers off the shelf without my permission, and that they are each drawing and writing. I give the class a five-minute writing assignment so I can deal with this table and bring the girls back into the fold.

I sit down at their table while they continue to draw and write. What's going on? I ask. Anat, in a friendly but intense voice, says, "Remember I told you that my older sister, Chris, died several years ago? I was away in camp when it happened, and she was drowned in a boating accident. Well, today is Chris's birthday, and I'm really missing her a lot. I'm making her some birthday cards and writing her a letter, and after school I'm going to go to the ocean and put these papers in the water."

Her friends at her table say, "And we are making cards and drawings too, to make Anat feel better, even though we didn't know Chris. We're feeling pretty sad with her. Do you think that's okay?"

Yes, I say.

I give the rest of the class a longer desk assignment, and I pick up the felt markers. "Dear Chris" I write, "I love having your sister, Anat, in my class. I wish I had known you too. Happy Birthday."

I postpone my Significant Lesson until tomorrow, when Anat and her friends can better receive it. I thank whatever spirits in my classroom helped me to set aside my annoyance.

Anat's parents divorced after Chris's death. Her father moved to Europe and started a new family, and Anat has never met these new brothers. She felt this loss deeply, and finally got enough courage to call her Dad and tell him that he needed to make a place for her, too, in his life. As a seventh grader, she was able to go to Europe and spend a summer with him and her new siblings.

The next year we celebrated a joyous event, when her mother remarried and delivered a baby son. Anat was at her side. Sitting at the table that day with Anat, making cards for her dead sister, helped me to better appreciate the significance of these events in her life.

I am teaching a Greek Mythology class. I order a movie about the Greek deities, but another movie arrives by mistake. This movie is called *The Living Stone*. I have seen it many times. It is a movie about Inuit life, and the title refers to the practice of carving stone in the long wintertime as elders tell the children stories. As the stories develop, the stone reveals the sea creature, the deity, or the hero who is the subject. It is a beautiful film about art and storytelling, but it is only loosely connected to Greek Mythology. I decide to show it anyway, as it is too late to get the movie I ordered in the first place. As we watch, I notice that the students are absorbed in the movie, but I feel a little guilty that I am deviating from our "real" subject. We don't talk much about the movie afterwards, as the class time is up, so I don't know what the students thought of it.

A few weeks later I run into a parent of one of the students in this Greek Mythology class. "Judy," she says, "thank you so much for showing that movie about the Inuits. Noah came home that day and told us that he didn't want anything for Christmas this year but stone-carving tools. He described the movie in great detail and then went immediately into the basement and started looking over some old stones we've had for years, carefully choosing one to carve. He's in the middle of this project now. He has a new-found passion in his life."

I thank her for telling me this. Some time later Noah brings his carving into his art class. It is a beautiful piece. Like the carvings in the movie, it is as if this figure were already alive in the stone, waiting for Noah to come along and carefully chip and file away its stone casing. We are amazed that this is Noah's first stone carving. Sometimes connected knowing happens by accident.

Today I run into Alivia's mother on the street. Alivia is a junior in high school now, and she has moved to Monterey to live with her father. Her mother tells me that she is rebellious and very suspicious of the authority figures in her life. She only goes to school part time, and can't wait to get out. "Since she left Dolores, she has had a lot of trouble," Alivia's mother tells me. "Some part of her has never returned to the classroom since she left your class."

I think about Alivia as a sixth grader. I remember how earnest she was, how sad that her only brother had left home to attend college, that her parents had just divorced, and that her mother was now at work when she comes home from school. She was very open about being lonely and confused. I recall her face with affection, and I think about a particular paper she wrote that led me to continue to assign a writing homework piece about a "food mistake." Since Alivia wrote this paper, I have read it aloud many times to students. Since we have all made food mistakes, either in cooking or in eating, I've had some great papers over the years.

When I get home from meeting Alivia's mother, I look for and find Alivia's food paper in one of my piles on the floor. Alivia wrote this piece after our International Holiday Pot Luck Luncheon, for which parents and students bring food from their ethnic backgrounds to share on the last day of school before winter break. Alivia's paper, which follows, is called "The Pot Luck."

Friday, December 20th, the last day of school, we had a potluck lunch. We all brought different things. I brought a Christmas log. For this story, we have to go back to Thursday night at seven p.m. I grabbed the cookbook, looked up desserts, and there it was: Christmas Log, or Gina's Nutroll. It called for 6 eggs, separated, ¾ cup of sugar, (which looked like it said 3¼ cups of sugar), 1¼ cups of nuts, 1 tsp. of baking powder, 1 tsp of vanilla, and two cups of whipping cream for the inside. After I read the recipe over, I checked over the ingredients and noticed that we needed whipping cream and nuts, so I called Sasha and put her on a leash. We ran up to the store and bought some whipping cream and nuts.

I ran home with one arm carrying the groceries and one with Sasha pulling and running too fast (especially if you have flip flops on). I got out everything and put it on the table. I got out one big bowl and two little bowls for the eggs. I also got the beater. I separated the eggs and beat up the egg whites till it was real thick and frothy. I then poured in the 3¼ cups of sugar (still not knowing it was supposed to be ¾ cups of sugar). The egg and sugar mixed up make it real glazy looking. So then I put it aside so I could mix up the egg yolks which I was supposed to put the sugar in.

I called my Mom to the kitchen and she told me I did it wrong and I was supposed to put the sugar in the egg yolks. So we put in all the other ingredients and tried to bake it but when we took it out of the oven it must have grown 4 inches tall! So we put it in the garbage.

Then we had to start all over. So I called Sasha and put her leash on. By then it was almost 9:00 at night. We walked up there to get eggs and more nuts. We scurried down to the house with me feeling more awful each step I took. Still not knowing about the sugar, I started all over again.

I knew not to put the sugar in the egg whites but in the egg yolks. I separated the eggs all over again. I beat up the egg whites making SURE I didn't put the sugar in. Then I beat the egg yolks and started pouring in the 3¼ cups of sugar and the nuts, vanilla, and the baking powder. It then got real hard, I mean hard!

I called my Mom to the kitchen and she read the recipe and saw that the 3¼ cups of sugar I put in was really only ¾ cups. I totally fell apart when she told me. I ran to my room (you really can't run to my room from the kitchen) and sat on my bed sobbing and sobbing. My Mom cleaned the kitchen. I was sad. I asked my Mom to call Ms. Logan and tell her the story. Ms. Logan told us that we didn't have to bring anything. Ms. Logan and my Mom talked for a while.

When my Mom got off the phone she told me she would make another Christmas Log. So, it was 10:45, and I called Sasha and put her on her leash and we walked up to the store and bought some more nuts. The owners must have thought we were very crazy to get so many bags of nuts! I brought them home with Sasha pulling me down the street thanking me for the walks I took her on. My Mom told me to go to bed and I did.

When I woke up, there in the kitchen was the cake put on the tin ready for the whipping cream to go on it and to be rolled up. My Mom walked in and told me to whip the cream. I said, "No way!!"

So my Mom whipped it up and she drove me to school. I took it to Room 217 where other people were dropping off their dishes. At 11:30 teachers and kids all took their plates and filled them up with delicious things. The potluck lunch was a great success.

As I re-read this paper I think about Alivia as a sixth grader, still connected to school, comfortable telling her story, able to share her mistakes with us. I remember the big hug she got when she came to my room with that precious dessert. I remember how much the class enjoyed hearing her paper read aloud. I hope that this sixth-grade Alivia is still alive in the angry Alivia who now hates school and can't wait to get out. I worry about what went wrong for her.

It is early in the semester, in September. I have planned to introduce the Names paper that day. In this assignment, I read a section from Alex Haley's *Roots*, where he describes how Kunte Kinte got his name. I read a portion of *Ishi, the Last of His Tribe*, that discusses the power of a name in the Native American community. I tell the story of Rumplestiltskin and I tell the story of my own name. The students then use dictionaries to look up the origins and meanings of their own names. They write a rough draft in class of everything they know about their own name (who named them, the meanings of their names, if they were named after someone, whether they would change their names if they could, what they would have been called if they born the other sex, whether they were called anything special when still in the womb, their nicknames and what they mean, etc.). The students then go home, read their papers to their parents, and ask for further information. The next day in class when I ask how many students learned something about their naming, almost all of them raise their hands.

I'm all ready with the materials and the energy to introduce this lesson in a big way, as in the past it has been a popular assignment. But on this day, before I begin, Lance looks up from the back of the room with a very concerned expression on his face. "I just lost my tooth," he mumbles, and I can see that he is on the verge of crying or smiling. "Congratulations!" I beam at him, and he decides to smile. "Would you like to go rinse your mouth out?"

"Yes." He does so and returns. "How many of you have lost a tooth this year?" I ask, and almost all hands go up. "How many of you have a loose tooth right now?" Some hands go up.

And in the interests of connected knowing, I switch lessons in mid-stream. Rumplestiltskin can wait. We do the tooth fairy lesson instead.

"What does your family do when you lose a tooth?" I ask. Many students eagerly volunteer stories about teeth under pillows turning to money. I tell the story of Latin American cultures that put children's teeth up into the rafters where the rats are, or down into gopher holes, so that the child's new teeth will grow in strong, like the rodents' teeth. What does it say about our culture that body parts can be exchanged for money?

(None of these lessons are original with me. I learned them all from the Bay Area Writer's Process workshops.)

"Tonight, for homework, describe the Tooth Fairy. Show me, through your writing, what the Tooth Fairy looks like."

"Can we make it into a story?"

"Yes. But you will be graded on your powers of description," I reply.

I get some fantastic writing the next day, which we read aloud in class. Funny, gruesome, winsome, clever—a whole parade of tooth fairies marches through our class. Some have dental -floss hair, some are like delicate ballerinas dressed in sparkling, glittering, fantasy clothing; some are radical, modern, far-out, and silly; some of them full of Scary Dentist Ferocity; one with George Washington's wooden false teeth on a string around her neck. Writing these Tooth Fairy stories lets my students hang on to the child in them, as they lose tangible parts of their babyhood and bravely face the unknown territory of adulthood. This assignment says that it is still okay to fantasize, to be silly, to hang on to their rituals.

Another day, we do our Names papers. These papers are also class favorites. By listening to the stories of each other's names, we learn many things about each other. I staple these papers onto a class bulletin board, and students often go to look at them on their way to sharpen pencils, or when they have a few free minutes. Seventh and eighth graders, former students of mine, come in eagerly to see the names papers and spend a lot of time at the bulletin board reading them. I have heard them smile at the newcomers and say, "Nice name paper," as a way of beginning a dialogue, establishing new friendships.

It is the last day of school. I'm sitting at my computer in my classroom, typing a final S.E.E.D report, an evaluation of my faculty development seminar on inclusive-curriculum, that will be published in a national newsletter. It is already a few days overdue. My niece, Hannah, is graduating from high school this afternoon, and I'm determined to get this report in the mail before I leave at one o'clock. Several of my students—Sharon, Frankie, Melissa, and Lia—are sitting on the carpeted floor engaged in intense discussion. Sharon is crying. I know these girls and I trust them to work out their conflict fairly. They continue to talk, argue, and cry. I continue to type.

Finally I say, "Is there something I can do to help?"

"Well," they tell me, "we want to cut our afternoon classes and go to the movies. Our parents said it was okay. After all, it is the last day of school and all the eighth graders are gone anyway. But Sharon is not sure she wants to. Well, she wants to go, but she wants us all to stay at school and go to the movies at three o'clock. But the matinee starts at two."

I know these students. They are good students, and I know their parents.

"Well, you have your decision-making list in your binders," I say. "Why don't you get it out and look at it? Use it. " This list helps them check various steps in decision-making—collecting information, predicting outcomes, checking for outside factors like peer pressure, etc..

I continue typing away at my report while they do this. They discuss each item on the checklist and how it is affecting their decision. Finally Frankie agrees to remain with Sharon at school, and join Lia and Melissa at the movies later. "Does this feel okay now?" I ask Sharon, who has stopped crying. "Yes," she says.

But a moment later Frankie says, "But isn't it also peer pressure if I am doing something that I don't want to do? I don't really want to stay with Sharon, I will do it because she is my friend, but I feel that it is peer pressure."

More tears.

"Sharon, "I ask, "why is it exactly that you don't want to go? Are you against cutting school in principle?"

"No," she says, "I'm just afraid."

"What exactly are you afraid of?"

"I'm afraid the principal will see us leaving and ask us what we are doing. I *really* want to go with them to the movies, and my parents said it's okay, I'm just afraid."

"What else are you afraid of?"

"Well, the movie is at the El Rey. I'm not sure how to get there."

I think about this. "And you're sure your parents said it was okay?"

"Yes," they assure me.

"I'm going to my niece's graduation in a few minutes. If you want to walk out of the building with me, that should solve one of your problems. And I can drop you off at the Castro Street muni station, and you can take the streetcar through the tunnel to the El Rey Theater. That should solve your second problem."

"Really? Will you do that?"

"Yes."

Sharon is relieved; the other three girls feel that they are no longer abandoning a friend in order to do what they want to do.

We walk down the hall, past the principal, who smiles at us, and leave the building. I am like the Pied Piper, leading children out of school.

A year later, Lia writes in my yearbook, "I will always remember your Shakespeare Class, the India class, Greek Mythology and the Writing Club, but mostly I will remember you leading children out of the building so they could cut the last day of school."

It is the third week of school. After class, Deborah, Anya, and Millie, three of my new sixth graders, stay after class and tell me they want to talk to me. "You are being unfair," they glower at me. "You don't call on us enough—you always call on the other kids. You don't read our papers aloud enough. You don't like us. You are playing favorites." I am upset to hear these complaints. I go back over the last three weeks, mentally, wondering if this is true. It doesn't feel true to me. I wonder what is really going on here. Clearly, these girls are mad at me.

I ask myself what is really wrong, and an answer presents itself. Each of these students is a younger sister of a much-beloved former student. Their big sisters have all graduated after spending three years in my classes. In fact, Jocelyn came to visit just last week, and got an enthusiastic welcome.

"I don't think this is about feeling that I don't like you," I say. "I think this is about your being afraid that I might not end up liking you as much as I like your older sisters. It is true, I am close to Missy, Jocelyn, and Ellie. I had them in my classes for three years. I know them better than I know you. I have only had you for three weeks. I don't expect you to be just like your sisters, but I expect that I will like you as much as I like them once I get to know you. I think your being mad at me right now is a way to protect yourself from the possibility that I won't like you enough. But you can relax. I like you already, and as we spend more time together, I'll like you even more. Please think about what I have said. I will also think about what you have said."

The girls are surprised. Anya recognizes some truth in it right away, and she stops to give me a hug before she leaves class for lunch. The other two take a little longer to come around, but the four of us end up having a good three years together. Millie, who is now in high school in Vancouver, is temporarily in San Francisco because her father is dying. She comes to our school frequently and spends time with us between visits to the hospital.

I am walking along Castro Street, and I run into Janet waiting at the bus stop. She is in her second year of high school and I haven't seen her for a while. We exchange greetings and hugs. "How is high school?" I ask her. "I don't know," she replies.

"What's wrong?"

"Well, everybody from our old school seems to be making new friends at Lowell. Things aren't the same."

"But, Janet," I ask, "aren't you making new friends too?"

"Yeah," she says slowly, "but it's hard."

I know Janet to be a talented, bright, outgoing person. I wait to hear what is wrong. She says, "I don't know, Ms. Logan, its just that at Lowell, well, nobody else's mother is gay."

"Oh," I say. "So, how is this for you?"

"It's really hard," Janet tells me. "Most of the kids I know I don't even talk to about it. But I finally made this one new friend in my gym class, so I told her, and, well, she was totally shocked, asking me really naive questions like, 'How did you get born?' It's all very depressing. Its not at all like middle school."

"Oh," I say, and we stay quiet for a while letting the truth of this hang between us. I try some words of comfort. "Well, Janet," I say, "at least you had that safe time, so now when people make naive or thoughtless comments, you know there is something wrong with *them* not something wrong with *you*."

Laura Burgess is an observer in my classroom, preparing for her student teaching assignment. She tell me about a curriculum class she is taking at San Francisco State University in which they read a choral poem about American history. "Every chorus started with the line, 'Now there was a man!'" Laura says. (It was a very Phase One poem.) Laura decides to write a play for her curriculum project. She does weeks and weeks of research, and writes *American Women Making History*. She turns the project in, gets an A, and generates a wonderful discussion about gender-inclusive curriculum among these future teachers.

Laura leaves us to begin student teaching in an elementary school. The students and I miss her, and we decide to perform her play and present it to her as a surprise, as she has written it and read it and discussed it but has never seen it.

We work hard learning the play. We create a big mural background that says American Women Making History by Laura Burgess. We gather hats and shawls for costumes. When we are finally ready, I invite Laura to our school for lunch. We buy a big bouquet of flowers and set it in the middle of the room on the floor, creating a stage area of sorts. We invite the principal and another sixth grade class to be our audience, but Laura has the chair of honor. We have a wonderful time performing Laura's play for her. She has created a piece full of women heroes, and it is amazing to me to watch my male students happily perform female roles. They don't mind being female when females are presented as valid, strong, important people. After the play we cry, "Author! Author!" and we give Laura the flowers.

This event is such a success that I begin to think about what to do next.

I call KALW, our local education radio station, and they send someone over to hear our play. He likes it, and schedules us to be on the radio for Women's History Month. The students are really excited about this project. They practice hard and do a professional job.

I introduce Laura to the women from the National Women's History Project in Santa Rosa, and they publish her play and put it in their catalogue. She has received royalties ever since.

The next year I arrange for my students to design a bookstore window display for Women's History Month. We continue to do this for several years. We have to work after school, and one year only boys volunteer for this assignment. I love watching them choose which materials to display, which student work to highlight, how best to arrange things to catch the eye of the public. We leave a blank notebook next to our display so that people can write their comments about it.

My friend Celeste, who has been in a long-term relationship with another woman, has decided to begin a family. Using the self-insemination program at UC Medical School, she is now pregnant with her first child. While I am visiting her one day, she asks me my opinion on whether or not I feel a child should ever be spanked. I tell her that I do not. We discuss this for a while, but she seems to still believe that an occasional swat on the behind for emphasis is an okay way to parent.

The next day I tell my sixth graders that my friend, Celeste, is about to become a parent for the first time, and that she is giving a lot of thought to her new role of motherhood. One of the things she is thinking about, I say, is whether or not a child should ever be spanked. She is collecting people's viewpoints in order to help her make a decision. "What did you tell her," the class asks. "I will tell you my reply," I say, "but first I would like to hear what you think. After all, I am not a parent, and it has been a long time since I have been a child."

As we discuss this, a woman walks in and sits down in the back of the room. I am used to having people observe my class and have many visitors between October and January, as parents of GATE students can choose the program they wish to send their child to.

The class discusses the issue of whether or not parents should spank their children. Then I ask the students to write Celeste a letter sharing their ideas and opinions with her. The class settles down to some intense writing; they take this role of adviser seriously and set out to convince Celeste that spanking is either okay or not okay.

I ask for volunteers to read their work aloud, and several read their letters. I listen carefully, learning something about each child's own home discipline system. When the bell rings and the students leave for lunch, I go to the back of the room and introduce myself to the woman who has been observing.

"What a great class," she says. "I wish I had had a teacher like you. My son will be coming to Dolores next year, and I wanted to see what your class was like. I think he will do fine here. He is not an easy child . . . he has had some difficulties in school . . . well, he is not really my son; I am his co-parent." I listen carefully as she decides how much she wants to tell me. Finally she says, "His mother and I are co-parents. We are a two-female family."

"Well," I say, "so is Celeste!" And we both laugh. I reassure her that several of our students come from gay families, and that we are committed to honoring all families.

When I give Celeste the stack of letters from the sixth graders, I feel that I am giving her a real gift—the points of view and opinions of children. And I feel that I have given the sixth graders a gift—an attentive audience for their personal ideas and opinions.

Frank, my colleague in the GATE program, is delivering some tests to a sixth-grade class. On his way out, he notices the doodlings of one of the students. "Why aren't you in my advanced art class?" he asks, and he gets the name and home-room of the student, Keishon White, 109. Keishon is glad to switch his elective into Frank's class, and Frank continues to recognize and honor his talent. Although Keishon doesn't test high, Frank arranges for him to enter the GATE program. He needs us, he tells me, and after all, GATE stands for Gifted and Talented, and Keishon is really talented. So Keishon spends the next two years in our program.

One day, as he is drawing a very sexy woman in Frank's art class, Hallie walks by, looks at it, and says, "That's not art, that's sexist trash." Frank puts the picture up on a bulletin board with a sign that says, Art? or Sexist Trash? at the top. The class discusses which it is, and why. Everyone who comes into the room over the next few days—parents, student monitors, other teachers, and the principal—is drawn into the discussion. Frank keeps a tally under each heading of how many people vote that way. It remains a running debate.

When Keishon graduates, he has a large portfolio of work. He applies to the McAteer School of the Arts and is accepted.

Some years later, Frank is at the DeYoung Museum, where some of his students are represented in a student art show. "Mr. Foreman, Mr. Foreman," someone calls out from the crowd. It is a very grown up Keishon, who is now a senior. "I have been meaning to visit you," he says. "I just got a full-time art scholarship to the Chicago Art Institute! I never knew I was an artist until I had your class. Now I have to go out into the world and be an artist, and I have you to blame," he teases.

These are the stories every teacher cherishes. This one is an example of the importance of the teacher as keen observer—if Frank had not taken the time to glance at Keishon's doodlings, or if he had been too lazy or distracted to do anything once he had seen them, Keishon's life might be very different today. The qualities that make exceptional teachers are not on any evaluation form that an administrator can check off; they cannot be measured by a standardized test. Yet lives are changed by such qualities.

I have a new student who has been in class only a few weeks. I have been concerned about her. She is the only Latina girl in the class, and I haven't noticed the other students making her feel as at home as I would like them to. There is something wild and wonderful about Wandia — she has an intense, angry energy. A slight accent makes her sometimes difficult to understand. One day, after lunch, she hauled off and hit one of the other girls, to get even for the fact that she was excluded from their lunch-ime game. Although I restrained her, I respected her up-front way of confronting these girls and the incident gave us a chance to talk about how everyone was feeling. Wandia's self-esteem was clearly intact, and she was not about to take anything from anybody. This, along with her sometimes unruly appearance, frightened some of the other girls, and they excluded her from their lunchtime games. They would cluster together and select a game to play, then chant, "Criss, Cross, Double Cross, Nobody Else Can Play But Us," before Wandia arrived. When she would arrive and ask to play, they would explain that the game was officially closed.

Today my sixth-graders are listening carefully to a presentation by the people from the Child Abuse Prevention program. The presenters are defining child abuse and teaching the class ways that they can protect and defend themselves. As I watch from the back of the room, I see Wandia begin to slump in her desk, her head in her hands. I move a little to the side of the room so I can see her face. I see a tear rolling down her cheek. I move to her side and take her by the hand, leading her to the big comfortable couch off to the side of the room. The rest of the class is involved in the presentation, but Wandia sits on the couch next to me and begins to cry. "Would you like to tell me about it?" I ask. She nods. While crying, she says, "It is hard for me to think about what they are talking about, because that is why I am here. We moved here to get away from my uncle, because my mother found out he was sexually abusing my younger sister. We ran away, but he is following us, and we are really scared. The other day when I was leaving school, I saw his truck. We are living over the garage of my grandmother's house until my mother can find a job. My sister cries all the time. She doesn't want to go to school."

She tells me more, then stops and looks at me, part defiant, part relieved, waiting to hear how I will receive this news. "It sounds to me like you could use a big hug," I say, and the defiant part goes away. She nods and she puts her arms around me and cries some more while I hold her. When she is finished we go together to see her counselor. We make sure her sister is getting therapy—yes, the whole family is in a program at General Hospital. She brings in a picture of her uncle and shows it to me and to her counselor. "Don't ever let this man take me," she says.

After this, she begins to share parts of her story in class. We are doing a nine-week unit on family life, and as we touch on topics that pertain to Wandia's situation, she talks about abuse. When she does this, it seems to me that the other students freeze, as in a film, and only Wandia and I continue to move and breathe and talk. When she finishes, the students unfreeze and it is as if nothing happened. They are unable to absorb her story. I hope that by deeply caring for Wandia, by accepting and supporting her story, my other students will be able to begin to identify with her.

I spend time with her each day. One Monday she comes to school distracted, teary, and unable to focus on her work. Her uncle had kidnapped her mother over the weekend, and tried to strangle her, but her mother had escaped. We have a restraining order, she tells me. "Are you feeling frightened?" I ask. "Not while I am in school," she says. "I keep my mind off it. But I am frightened when I am at home." She tells me that her sister sits on the floor of the bathroom with her head on the toilet seat cover, and cries all the time. "We got her one of those fuzzy covers for the toilet, to make her feel better," she says.

She and her mother plan a surprise birthday party for her sister. Wandia is excited and enthused. When she returns after the weekend of the party, I ask her how it went. "Fine, until my sister's friend got shot." "What do you mean?" I ask. I remember reading in the newspaper that a young girl was killed in a random shooting while walking along the street. "She shouldn't have walked by those projects," Wandia says.

I am teaching the same Family Life unit to the seventh and eighth graders in the afternoon. This is a class for everyone who didn't get family life in the sixth grade—either because they were in another teacher's class who didn't do it, or they transferred in from another school. I distribute a Dear Abby-type letter in class. This letter is written by a seventeen-year-old girl. In it she says that she and her boyfriend are thinking of having sexual intercourse. They both will be going to college in the fall, and it is unthinkable to them that she might get pregnant. Nevertheless, they seem to be getting closer and closer to having sexual intercourse.

The assignment is for the students to read the letter and then to write a careful answer. After some writing time, I ask students to share their answers with the class. Most answers involve detailed instructions about various birth control methods, the significance of nonoxynol-nine, where to purchase birth control devices, how to use them, and admonishments about never having sex without using a condom. Melissa raises her hand. "But the girl writing this letter said she was just *thinking* about having sex," Melissa says, "She didn't say she was *going* to have sex. Why is everyone talking about birth control when all she said was that she was thinking about it? When I am flying in an airplane, I *think* about what it would be like to open the cabin door and watch all the papers, seats and people be sucked out of the plane, but I would never *do* it."

For Melissa, having sex is as preposterous and as dangerous as opening a plane door at 32,000 feet. On the other hand, Kerry asks to speak to me after class. We go to sit on the couch so we can be comfortable and so I can give her my full attention. This classroom couch is a time-out place, and the unwritten law is that when we sit on the couch, we become two human beings, instead of one teacher and one student. We also become invisible to the rest of the class, so that it is okay to cry, complain, laugh, or lie down for a nap. The class continues on. But it is now after school, and Kerry and I are alone.

"I don't like this class," she tells me. "I want to switch classes."

"Okay. Tell me why."

"This class is going to be about whether or not to use drugs, whether or not to have sex. I already have a lot of experience with drugs, and I have a lot of experience with sex, so I think this class will be boring for me."

"Hmm. I see your point. But I disagree with you. You weren't here on the first day of school when I talked about the plans for this class, but you should know that I see my responsibility as your teacher is to bring in all the latest information on sexually transmitted diseases, on birth control methods, on AIDS, and on other subjects. We will have about twenty guest lecturers in this class, and each lecturer will be an expert in his or her field. It seems to me that this is the perfect class for you. As a sexually active person you deserve all the latest information you can get. Also, Kerry, this class is about making choices and decisions. If you have strong feelings and a lot of experiences, it seems to me that you can be a great resource for the rest of the class. Also, choices and decisions are never final—we continue making them all of our lives. You might even find that this class influences you to change your mind about some things."

She thinks about what I have said. "It's not really that," she says. "What it really is is that I am jealous of the other kids. They have parents who care about what they do and who watch out for them. I've never had anybody really watch out for me. Now that I am in therapy, I understand that I should have had a lot of parenting that I never got. It will be painful for me to be in this class."

"You've done a lot of work in therapy in a very short time," I tell her. "I am really moved that you are able to articulate how you are really feeling. I am proud of you. You will be an asset to this class. I wouldn't want to do it without you."

Kerry stays in Family Life. We have two evening sessions for students and their parents. Kerry attends both sessions, and I act as her parent.

There are thirty-two students in this class. Each student has a story (as I write this I hear the music from *Dragnet* in the background—dum da dum dum). I told one of Melissa's stories and one of Kerry's to illustrate how different they are. One curriculum does not fit all. When teachers complain about class size increasing, they are really lamenting their growing inability to learn each child's story and to tailor the curriculum in such a way as to fit the needs of each one. The more children in a class, the more necessary it is to have just one story. But how can one curriculum respond to both a Melissa and a Kerry? The answer, I think, is that they both get left out.

Kathie, who shares my classroom with me, has a particularly needy student named Emilio. Small for his age, dark-haired, and shy, one day he says to her, "Teacher, today it is my birthday." Kathie gives him a big hug, she wishes him a happy birthday, and she gives him special privileges for the day. Emilio sits smiling and pleased. A member of a very large family with few financial and emotional resources, Emilio is too often overlooked at home. Three or four weeks later, Emilio says shyly, "Teacher, today it is my birthday." Kathie gives him special birthday attention. Every four or five weeks during the remainder of the year, Emilio announces his birthday. Kathie, who teaches math, never points out to him that it is impossible to age seven or eight years during seventh grade. There is little she can do about his home life. But in school, she keeps on giving those hugs.

5. American Women Making History

When my niece, Hannah, was twelve years old, that age when young girls feel the need to separate from mothers and other significant female role models, she announced to me with a trace of defiance, "Auntie Judy, I know that you are a feminist, and I feel that I should tell you that I am not one."

Now, Hannah and I have always been close, and I have always been one of her confidants. She telephones me to read me her writing before she turns in her homework, and I am one of her biggest fans. She calls me to complain when her older brother doesn't do his share of cleaning the bathroom. When she argues with her stepmother, I listen to her side of the story.

"Really, Hannah," I say. "What has brought you to the decision that you are not a feminist?"

Hannah pauses. "Well," she says, "I guess I'm not one because I don't really know what it means."

"It would certainly be a mistake," I say, "to describe yourself as something when you are not sure what it means. Actually, many people define *feminist* in many different ways. The definition I use when I talk about it in the classroom is that a feminist is a man or a woman who believes that both males and females should have equal rights and responsibilities in both the public and private domains, and who is willing to act on those beliefs. In other words, not only should you be able to run for president of the United States just as easily as your brother, Josh, but he should have equal responsibility for cleaning up the bathroom you two share."

Hannah pauses a moment to let this sink in.

"I am one," she declares. And she has been, ever since.

I tell this story because I think a lot of students, and other people too, come to the classroom with misinformation about what it means to have a feminist classroom, or to include women in the curriculum. Like Hannah, they distance themselves from what they don't understand.

When I present workshops on the middle-school feminist curriculum, I am always asked questions like, "But what do the *boys* do while you are sewing quilts?" Or they ask, "But how do the boys in the classroom respond when you are studying women?" To me, these questions indicate many misconceptions.

First of all, for many, many years women have benefited in schools by studying the lives, values, and experiences of men. I think men can benefit just as much from studying about the lives, values, and experiences of women. Women's lives need to be presented without apology. They need to be presented as one half of the world's experience. It is only when they are presented as "lesser," that boys don't want to do it. And when they are presented as "lesser," girls don't want to do it either. And I don't blame them.

But my audience persists. "Don't the boys *ever* object?" they want to know. So to make them feel better, I tell them the story of Pablo, who did object.

Pablo was the third son in a single parent family, and I had had his older brother Chris in my class some years before. Pablo was a sixth grader when we were doing a fairly sophisticated comparative study of the lives of women in Saudi Arabia, Israel, the United States, and Sweden We began by looking at how women achieved power and status in these countries, and from there we proceeded to look at many aspects of each culture, from family law to religious values.

One evening Pablo's mother telephoned, shortly after I had sent home an interim warning informing her that Pablo was missing several homework assignments. I was glad to hear from her, and frankly, I thought she was calling to thank me, as the day before Pablo and three other boys had come to my home for a tea party. We baked cookies and had a nice visit, and I drove them each home since it was raining rather hard.

I was unprepared for her anger. She asked me if I was teaching what I "was supposed to," since Pablo had complained to her that we were studying about women. She was concerned that he wouldn't learn the "real curriculum." I replied that Pablo was indeed learning the "real curriculum," and that if she sat down and talked to him about what we were doing, I thought she would find solid lessons there in history, comparative religion, etc. But, I explained, we are entering these lessons through the female experience, so actually Pablo is having something added to his education, not something subtracted. By focusing on how women gained status in these four countries we learned about family life, public policy regarding women and children, and the value of keeping house and raising children, as well as about the public world of government, finances, and so forth.

California's Mentor Teacher Program funds districts to select up to 2% of their teachers to receive a $4,000 a year bonus to reward good teaching and to keep good teachers in the classroom. My district uses this money to provide extra pay for extra work. My mentor contract called for me to collect, develop, and use materials on women. I explained that as a student of a mentor teacher, Pablo was part of a pilot program in my class. "Actually, Pablo is very lucky," I say. "He's getting something extra. Most curriculum today still includes only the male perspective."

But I agree to her request for a conference "with the school counselor and the principal." We arrange a time and place for the conference. Pablo's mother leaves me with the distinct feeling that I am "in trouble." I hang up the phone and unplug it, wanting no more parent conferences that night, thank you. I feel sorry for myself. Here I am, baking cookies, driving kids home in the rain, knocking myself out not to be just a textbook teacher, and this is what I get. I soak in a hot tub and plan "my side" of the impending conference, since it already feels like an unfriendly win/lose ordeal.

About ten-thirty, I plug the phone back in and it immediately starts ringing. I am surprised when I hear Pablo's mother. "I am so glad you answered the phone," she says. "I have called to apologize. I did as you suggested. I sat down and talked to Pablo about what he has been doing in your class. You are right, he is learning many things that are important. And he is also learning about women's lives and experiences. Here I am, a working mother trying to raise three sons, and you are teaching about me, about my life. I am so sorry I gave you a bad time. I hope you will forgive me."

I am friendly on the phone and "forgive her," and inside I think to myself, don't forget this moment. A bit ago you felt *awful*. Now you feel *terrific*. Pablo's mother was unsupportive only because she didn't understand. She wants to cancel our appointment, but I encourage her to keep it so we can help Pablo get his work in.

At the time, Pablo was a difficult child, and needed both his mother and his teacher to help him mature. I had Pablo for three years, and in many ways he did grow up. But I never forgot that early experience, which started out feeling so unpleasant, and ended up feeling so good. A few days before his graduation from middle school, I asked Pablo if I could interview him about his experiences at school. He seemed delighted. I asked him many questions, one of which was, "Now that you are going to high school, you may or may not have teachers that include women in curriculum. If they do not, do you think you would ever choose to do reading or research on women if it were not an explicit part of the assignment?"

"Oh, sure," Pablo responds easily. "Especially on Demeter. Demeter's stories are my favorite."

Pablo's story has echoed my niece Hannah's.

I think that some people are afraid that because (men's) history excluded women for so long, that somehow women's history is about excluding or replacing men, which it is not. I am aware, however, that by focusing on women for two or three assignments a year (the NOW essay contest and the quilt), and by including women in many other assignments (Black History Month), I am seen as very extreme, whereas many teachers focus only on men's experience for the entire year, and this is seen as "normal."

If my class seems anxious at the beginning of a "woman's unit," I reassure them that women's studies is not about "ruling over," it is about "existing with." It is not about competing to see who is better, on top, or more valuable. It is important to be explicit with these reassurances right away. Feminist teaching is not about allowing a win/lose situation to develop between boys and girls. It is not about the girls winning or the boys winning.

I teach my sixth grade class for three periods in the morning—Language Arts, Reading, and Social Studies. In the afternoon, I teach seventh and eighth graders, half of whom are my former sixth graders, for a two-period block of English/ Social Studies core. Sometimes a unit lasts for a whole semester, sometimes for nine-weeks. Since I team plan with three other teachers, we have a lot of flexibility in our scheduling. We like combining the seventh and eighth graders as it gives us more choices in meeting their needs.

One year we focus on Global Studies, the next year we focus on American Studies. So each student gets everything, eventually. But as seventh and eighth graders, they can, with parental guidance, choose which teacher and which unit suits them best. During the American Studies year, I teach a five-week, two-hour-a-day class called American Women Making History.

I begin with a lot of concerns about this class. How can I, in five weeks, do justice to the regional, ethnic, racial, economic and cultural diversity of women in American history? How can I include women from all aspects of life—private and public—so that students expand their notions of what history is? How can I cover not only the last two hundred years, but the hundreds of years before that that women lived and worked on this soil? How can I make this class fun and exciting so that students will internalize a love of history and research that will not self-destruct in five weeks?

Fortunately, because I have been a mentor teacher for the last several years and have had a supplementary budget for materials, I have many books by and about women in my classroom. In fact, when students enter my room for the first time, they often look around at all the shelves and displays of books, and ask meekly, "Are we going to have to read all this?"

I quickly explain that my classroom is a resource center for other teachers and students, and that while they are free to read and use the books in the room, they certainly will not be expected to read them all.

I have collected many examples of curriculum from other districts. Assuredly I could keep them mighty busy reading, writing, and memorizing for the next five weeks. But I don't want my students to be consumers of curriculum. I want them to be producers of curriculum.

In each class, I have students with a diversity of interests, abilities, talents, learning styles, and something that I think in Kindergarten they call "emotional readiness." What works for one student doesn't necessarily work for another. When I think of curriculum, I picture a journey. In traditional curriculum, everyone is supposed to be on the same journey at the same time, and the teacher's role is like that of a sheep dog, trying to keep everyone together. It is like being on a field trip, always looking ahead to one group of students and saying, "Wait for us, don't get on that streetcar, we're not all there yet," and then looking behind, saying, "Hurry up, walk faster, we'll never get there at this pace."

But I think of feminist curriculum as a journey that acknowledges that, while everyone needs to be moving forward, most of us are in different places at different times. Some people are filling out passport applications; some people are touring beautiful Cathedrals and famous monuments; some people are sitting in cafes having bread and cheese and intense conversations; some people are learning Japanese; some are homesick, writing letters home; some are putting together their photo albums. The teacher's role in this vision becomes one of keen observer. After all, it is inappropriate to speak Japanese to someone who is filling out a passport application, and it is inappropriate to hand a photo album to someone eating and visiting in a cafe. This metaphor seems to capture my impression of the difference between traditional teach-and-test curriculum, and student-centered curriculum that acknowledges the individual interests, talents, and learning styles in the class.

Thinking about one of my curriculum guidelines—if I control the content, you get to control the form; if I control the form, you get to control the content—I decide to make the content (women in history) the "have to" part of the class, and the form the "get to" part of the class.

So I talk to the students about the project they will be doing in this class. They may work alone or in a group of not more than four. They may choose one aspect of women in history to research in depth, such as women in sports or drama or dance or social reform. Or they may choose to research one group of women's experience, such as Chinese immigrants to California, or the Filipina American experience. Or, they may focus on one time frame or region, like Women in the West.

The students must first research their topic in depth, then present their findings to the class in a way that allows us to share what they have learned. We will each be both teacher and learner. We won't pretend to cover it all. The class presentation may include a dramatic skit; it may take the form of a comic book, a mural, a board game, a children's book, complete with illustrations, and so forth.

We spend some time discussing our options. I show slides of former student presentations for inspiration. Some students know immediately what they want to do. Others need more guidance. When students come up with ideas for their own projects, I try to say yes.

Now, students at this age (at any age, really) may look askance at women in history (the "have to" part), but they are suckers for making comic books, playing music, painting murals, and acting out (the "get to" part). When they hear that they can include art, drama, and music, they are hooked. Suddenly this sounds like fun. We go to the local libraries and the school libraries, and discover that they don't have as many books on women as our classroom does. The students are shocked. They begin to understand that something is being left out.

I help them narrow down their topics into reasonable chunks, and they begin scanning indexes and tables of contents for information. We talk about primary research, and they begin to set up interviews. Students work in small groups around the room. Some sit on the floor reading quietly. Others go behind the filing cabinets to rehearse skits. Others are making puppets, painting murals, cutting things out. I devote about a third of the class time to this research and project activity. During the other two thirds I read to them. I show videos and movies, most ordered from Project SEE (Seeking Educational Equity) in Sacramento, a branch of the state government committed to providing audio-visual materials about women to classrooms. Teachers can order materials by phone for a specific date and pay only for return postage. This way I am able to show movies like *One Fine Day*, *Rosie the Riveter*, *Women of Summer*, and *Still Killing Us Softly*. Students begin to expand their notions of women in history beyond Betsy Ross.

We talk about what is "real work." I tell them about Peggy McIntosh's theories of including women in curriculum. We begin to use her terminology in class. A simplification of her Phase Theory hangs on the wall of our classroom. I show segments of videos relating to their projects. We read poems, letters, and short stories written by women of color. I show video segments of *Famous Americans* on Elizabeth Cady Stanton, Susan B. Anthony, Soujourner Truth, Harriet Tubman, Eleanor Roosevelt, Elizabeth Blackwell, Margaret Sanger, Helen Keller, Georgia O'Keeffe, and others. We listen to songs about Sybil Ludington, Harriet Tubman, and Gertrude Ederle.

We listen to the music of Sweet Honey in the Rock, a group of African American women who sing about black experience, and we discuss the lyrics. We ask ourselves, who are we leaving out?

In the fourth week, we begin our class presentations. It is time to teach each other, and at this stage in the unit I am unprepared for how wonderful the students' projects are. Most presentations are much longer than I expected. In the end, I usually have to ask the other three teachers for an extra two days before we switch classes.

In this unit, some students do a traditional oral presentation of a research report on one outstanding woman such as Eleanor Roosevelt or Sojourner Truth. That indicates that for these students, school means carefully fulfilling someone else's expectations. But most students somehow put their own creative signature on their projects.

Hallie has created several small cardboard statues of liberty, holding up the freedom flame. On the face of each, she has pasted the picture of one of the women on whom she is reporting. She holds up each statue as she tells the story of that woman's life: Sarah Winnemucca, holding a book that says "Indian Rights"; Barbara Jordan, holding a book that says "Civil Rights"; Mother Jones, holding a book that says "Workers' Rights"; Sojourner Truth, holding a book that says "Women's Rights"; and finally, with flame-colored hair, Cyndi Lauper, holding a book that says "Individual Rights."

Anat and Diane have taken a cardboard box and constructed a television set. They have used a long piece of paper, wound around two dowels, to turn the images on the "screen." Their topic is women in literature, and they talk about Tillie Olsen, Virginia Woolf, Kate Chopin, Alice Walker and Willa Cather.

Another student has also constructed a television set out of a box. He reports on Amelia Earhart as he turns the paper on the "screen." We see Amelia's baby footprint, her first plane with a price tag on it, a map of the United States tracing her first cross-continental journey.

Four of my male students have put many hours into constructing a Jeopardy game on Women in History. Students are delighted and respond favorably to $50, $500, and $5,000 questions. The boys have spent their own money on candy prizes.

Four female students have set up a Judy Chicago *Dinner Party*, drawing the faces of several women on paper plates, placing cards next to the setting, and talking about these women's lives as the class walks around their table.

Dan and Abraham, our class artists, work together on a comic book called, "Two Women Written Back Into History," about Harriet Tubman and Sojourner Truth. They are proud of their work and share it eagerly with the class. I photograph them.

Annette and Zoe come up with another original project. Struck by the quote from the UN Decade of Women that frames one of my classroom walls ("Women are one-half of the world's population, they do two-thirds of the world's work, they earn one-tenth of the world's income, they own one-hundredth of the world's property"), they borrow a video camera from Annette's uncle. Each Saturday, they go to one or two different neighborhoods in the city, planning carefully to visit a diversity of neighborhoods. They take turns "manning" the camera while the other acts as interviewer and politely asks strangers on the street if they will help with a homework assignment. If the subject agrees, the interviewer states the UN statistics and ask for a response. Most people have never heard the statistics before, and respond with interest, telling personal stories about why they think the figures are accurate. Most are delighted with the assignment. "I never got to do anything like this when I was in school," is a frequent comment .

Watching this video takes a long time. Annette and Zoe have not learned about editing. They are both novices, so the resulting footage is sometimes a bit wobbly. But their enthusiasm for this project infects the class, and we spend several class days watching and talking about the footage. "Wait until you see what happened in the financial district," they tell us. And sure enough, at one of the convention centers, a bus pulls up, and Zoe asks the tourists to respond to the quote. One man is pretty intoxicated and he uses this opportunity to impress his friends by saying some ugly and oppressive things about women. He goes on and on. He does not swear, but he says terrible things.

The girls bravely keep on filming.

"How did you feel when this was happening?" I ask the girls.

"We couldn't *believe* that he was saying such things, but we were so excited to be getting footage of it! We knew just telling you about it wouldn't work—we wanted the class to be able to *see* it." Like professionals, they didn't let their personal feelings interfere with taping the interview.

Zeb, a student I have been worried about for sometime because he skims over his work and doesn't connect with assignments, makes a board game on Harriet Tubman. He has a great time doing it. But the game cards say things like "the sheriff found you in the swamp, go to jail." Or, "Whoops, you took a wrong turn, forfeit your chance to go north." The artwork is nice, I say to Zeb, but it doesn't reflect Harriet Tubman's real life. She was never caught—she never lost a passenger. She never had to go to jail. Zeb did the "get to" without doing the "have to" (in this case, proper research). Zeb fails the assignment.

Years later, his mother will describe me to a friend as "a flaming feminist."

Other students construct board games. One is on Women in the Olympics, and students have little cardboard female biological signs (circles with a plus) for markers.

Amelia decides to do a report on the Triangle Shirtwaist Fire. She does extensive research and ties the incident into the larger theme of workers' rights and social reform. At the same time, she constructs a large model of the Triangle building. With yellow and red paper she depicts fire coming out of the windows on the top three floors. Her report is dramatic and effective.

Some time later, I run into Amelia's mother, who is also a teacher, at the local supermarket. She tells me that her husband is an architect, and that while her son had often worked with his dad in his office, this project was the first time that Amelia had done so. As she made her miniature building, Amelia learned to use his tools and talked to him about his skills.

Students begin to get a sense of the richness of women's studies. They say things like, "Why didn't I ever hear of her before?" Or, "How come this isn't in the books?" They get all kinds of ideas from each other. Sometimes my giving verbal permission isn't enough—they need to see other students doing art projects or videotapes, before they get a sense of what it can look like. Sometimes once they see what other students have done, those students who write traditional essays on one woman ask to do their project over.

The year we are centering on American Studies, I offer other elective classes: American Poetry, American Biographies, American Short Stories. Before each class, I consider how to include Phase Four curriculum. In the poetry class, for example, I include many poems by women.

Rosie is intrigued with the poem, "Two Gretels," by Robin Morgan. She decides she would like to paint a watercolor of this poem. Since she is in my homeroom every morning, I invite her to bring her watercolors to class, and to use the fifteen minutes every morning that we spend on sustained silent reading (this is school policy—everyone from janitors to students is supposed to read quietly during this time) to paint instead. None of the other students complain as Rosie works diligently each day on her painting. They continue to read quietly. Rosie produces a lovely work of art. Her art teacher and I frame it for her, and give it to her for a graduation present.

I want to say a word here about saying yes to the passions of individual students. I can hear someone saying, But all the children are supposed to be reading, why should *one* be allowed to paint? Shouldn't they *all* be allowed to paint if Rosie gets to? Perhaps this critical voice that I hear is my own and maybe that's why I need to pause a moment to answer it. My response is that students seem to understand that by saying yes to one student's needs, I am in a way saying yes to all their possibilities too. Unlike some adults, they seem to understand that everyone has different interests, needs, talents, abilities, and gifts. I would be remiss if I let the whole class paint during sustained silent reading. After all, the Curriculum Committee has voted that this is what we are supposed to be doing during this time. But I don't feel remiss in letting Rosie paint. She is a straight-A student who already reads a great deal. But with her demanding schedule, this painting will not come to life without this gift of time. The students in her class understand this.

Rosie's painting is an example of what can happen when teachers give students permission to follow their own visions. This philosophy also enables students to include their own stories in their work. Children of all ages need to feel connected to what they are doing, either by being allowed to discuss their own experiences and feelings, or by being allowed to express what they have learned in a way that is meaningful to them, as in art or drama.

In the American Biographies class, we begin with biographies of people in our own families. Students interview and write about their grandparents, parents, or aunts and uncles, and do an oral report in class as well as a written report. We learn about grandmothers and assorted family members.

Ellie tells of her Irish grandmother in Brooklyn who, distressed that her oldest son had married a non-Catholic girl, one day spontaneously baptised her two granddaughters in the kitchen sink.

Anat tells us about her Jewish grandmother in Brooklyn. She was making chicken soup one day, as her several children played on the kitchen floor. The laundry was hung out to dry off the fire escape, and someone on the roof of the tenement threw away a lighted cigar, which landed on the laundry and set it on fire. Anat's grandmother thought quickly and doused the fire with the chicken soup.

Hua writes about his father, who whose name is Tac Tran. He describes his father's education, his career as an English teacher, the Vietnam War, and his family's escape by boat in the middle of the night. They were rescued by an Indonesian ship after five days on the open seas, just as their food and water were running out. After some time in a refugee camp, they came to San Francisco, where they first stayed in an uncle's basement in Daly City. Eventually, they found a place of their own, and Hua's father now teaches English in a high school in San Francisco.

Students learn a lot from this American Biographies class, and Hua's story becomes a window to help us experience his life with him. Later, Hua is elected student body president of our school.

The stories are too numerous for me to report here. But the assignment gives students opportunities to interview and celebrate members of their own families, and as we learn more about each other, we like each other better.

We also learn more about ourselves. Ellie, who wrote about her Irish grandmother, comes back to visit after graduation. I am applying for something or other, and I ask her to write me a letter of recommendation. In this letter, among other things, she says that while she knew her maternal grandmother well, this assignment had given her the opportunity to find out about her paternal grandmother, and to claim a part of her heritage that had been in the shadows.

I particularly enjoy teaching American Short Stories, and find that this class gives me lots of opportunities for Phase Four curriculum. For example, we read Maureen Daly's award-winning story, "Sixteen," and discuss it in class. The students love it. I ask them to write a story with their own age as the title, and to capture the spirit of their own age in the same way that Maureen Daly has captured the spirit of being a sixteen-year-old girl.

Hallie, Rosie's younger sister, writes the following story:

Twelve

Buddy Holly crooned in the darkened room. Ninth and eleventh graders flirted and fought. A couple slammed a door behind them. It was an end-of-school party, and I had somehow been cool enough to get invited.

The bright birds at the party were two sophisticated McAteer boys, in black suits (it was formal), slicked back (or up, as the case may be) hair and long, thin cigarettes. After standing around for a time, self-consciously talking and preening with the older kids, one of the "smoothies" asked me to dance.

Surprised, I went out and we danced, long and close. It was quite a different experience from dancing with bashful junior high boys. Afterwards, I sat down, legs crossed just right, and we talked softly for awhile. Then, (Heaven!), we danced again. He stood with his arm around me. I was confused. Was he just fooling around? Did he like me? I responded eagerly, and after a time we were "an item" at the party.

I'm afraid I looked at him adoringly the whole time. As we stood in the darkened hallway outside of the dancing room, he asked me my name. I had forgotten to tell him. His arm was comfortable and familiar, the lights soft and shiny, Buddy Holly's voice sweeter than ever.

"Anna," I said softly.

"Hey, you're Amy's sister!" I nodded. "I thought she said her sister was twelve!"

I sighed, and came out of the softness of this fantasy. His arm was gone, the lights seemed to reflect in their glare all my youth and inadequacy, and Buddy Holly sounded resentful as if he, too had been deceived.

"That's me," I said quietly. He didn't act shocked or angry, he just casually moved away. I realized that with all his sophistication and experience, it meant nothing to him. While I, with all my pent-up adolescence that had been waiting so long, set free and shot down, I was crushed. And so comes the great change. I no longer have rosy images of romance under friendly stars, and the pain is dulled, but I will never feel the same.

Not everyone writes such a descriptive piece. But, everyone thinks about and writes about the quintessence of being eleven or twelve.

We read Alice Walker's "Everyday Use," and Dorothy Canfield's "The Bed Quilt." Students write about artifacts of family history in their homes. Each story offers us an opportunity to write about aspects of ourselves.

The next year is spent on global history. During this year I have taught many classes in Greek Mythology, as well as units on India, Southeast Asia, Shakespeare, Fairy Tales, Rites of Passage, and Victorian novels. Each class combines reading, writing, research and social studies. As I teach each class, I continue to think about inclusive curriculum and Peggy McIntosh's phase theory.

In one class, I use Anne Kent Rush's *Moon, Moon* for a text. This book is a collection of facts, poems, stories, fables, myths, articles and essays about the moon. Ms. Rush's contention is that any given society's attitudes towards the moon also reflect their attitudes about women. She collected all the information about the moon from as many cultures around the world as she could. We discuss this theory in class, and decide to explore her ideas and test them for ourselves. Our homework is to look at the moon every night. We talk about everything from lunacy to the dimensions of moon craters. We also agree to do a special project about the moon. Meanwhile, class time is spent reading poetry, stories, myths, and science, and writing our own stories, poems and myths about the moon. A parent drops by to visit. She happens to be an expert astrologer and tarot card reader. She stays to talk about the moon in astrology.

Natis, an intense, bright, highly verbal student who seems years older than twelve, constructs a wonderful mobile. Enameled discs hang properly depicting the phases of the moon—waxing, full, waning, and dark. Nan, tall for her age, big-boned and sturdy, sews a moon goddess costume. It is a long dark blue gown with seed pearls sewn onto it. Her close-fitting blue cap with its silver satin stuffed new moon, stands straight up like a crown on her straight, light brown hair. I am surprised, because Nan is so shy, but she wears this costume to class with great dignity. Lisa, her dark, curly hair spilling over her shoulders, shares the songs she has collected and taped: "Moon Over Miami," "Blue Moon," "Shine On Harvest Moon," "How High the Moon." Some of the best student short stories I've ever read come out of this class. This class reminds me that curriculum does not have to be either/or, as in either science or art, either facts or fantasy, but can be both/and, as in both about space and about ourselves, both about learning and about having fun.

6. Angela's Ritual

One year when planning electives in English and Social Studies with a global emphasis, I decided to teach a class called Rites of Passage. My intention was to develop a class that honored the middle-school child's need to understand the role of ritual in daily life, and to introduce each student to a cross-cultural awareness of how humans celebrate universal events such as birth, coming of age, marriage, healing, holidays, and death.

Since this class was to be about researching and experiencing ritual, I began with an initiation ritual, initiating the students into the class. I asked them to bring an object that they cherished to class. We moved the chairs and tables aside, sat in a circle on the carpeted floor, and began by going around the circle, giving each student an opportunity to put her/his cherished object in the middle of the circle, telling us what it was and why it was special. I explained, as best I could, the Native American belief in the power of the four directions, and we honored the power of the East, South, West, and North. We lit a candle to represent fire, incense to represent air, and we had a bowl of water and a rock and flowers to represent earth.

I asked the students to go around the circle and talk about different groups they belonged to, or different roles that were a part of their make-up. For example, I began, "I am a teacher, a friend, a daughter, a sister, a union member, an aunt." Each student defined herself/himself ("I am a Boy Scout, forward on the basketball team, a member of the Filipino Club."). Then I said that we were also now members of this class. Look around the room, I said, we will be together like a kind of family for nine weeks. We will never be together in quite this same way again. We each have our unique, individual selves, and we are each now part of this group. To ritually represent these ideas, I brought a large skein of red yarn. We went around the circle, and each student wrapped this yarn around the left wrist of the person sitting on her left. "This is to represent that you are woven into this group," she said. When we were all looped together, I then passed around a pair of scissors, and as each student cut the yarn for the person on her left, she said, "This is to represent that you are also unique, you are your own person." I finished by suggesting that they tie a knot in their red-yarn bracelet, and wear it throughout our time together as a tangible symbol of our class. They did so.

I was surprised myself at the power of this ritual. I don't think I've ever seen a class focus and bond so quickly. This ritual was to initiate you into this class, I told them. The next assignment was to group themselves into no more than six-person groups, and decide what rite of passage they would be responsible for researching. Our task was to look at many cultures, and to report our findings back to class. The second part of this assignment was to provide some kind of ritual for the class that embodied the group's research. This ritual could involve food, music, guided fantasy, etc.

It has been eight years since I taught this class, but I have vivid memories of the commitment of the students, the rituals they provided, the wealth of information they collected. Each group presented a formal research report as well as a ritual. One group researched daily life rituals—how different cultures treated the cooking and serving of food, getting up and going to bed, saying hello and saying good-bye, greeting guests, etc. One group researched seasonal holidays, and we had groups on birth, death, marriage, coming of age, and mental or physical crises.

Lea was one of my best students. She had lost one of the members of her household to AIDS, and she had other family friends who were dying of AIDS. She was the chair of the death group. Not only did she do significant research on a variety of attitudes and customs about death in the USSR, Mexico, China, some African tribes, Japan and Ireland, but she led us in a very powerful ritual where she took us on a guided fantasy and asked us to imagine our own deaths. I admit this made me nervous. I was afraid some of my students might become frightened or upset. So when the guided fantasy was over, I asked that we go around the circle and check in, telling something about how we were feeling, or how the experience was for us. I was amazed at how calm and clear everybody was, and how their "death experience" reflected something about who they already were. Heidi, for example, was still a very playful pre-adolescent. "I imagined myself on a fluffy, comfortable cloud," she reported, "happily bouncing up and down, and looking down on earth at all my friends and family, knowing I could play tricks on them." Nobody was upset or scared. This class taught me to trust this process more than I already had.

Rosie designed a coming of age greeting card. She painted a picket fence with a pink rose bush growing on one side, about to turn a corner. This watercolor painting had a poem inside:

> How quickly the years have passed
> Since I first planted my little rose bush.
> She was frail and delicate and

> We weren't always sure
> She'd make it through winter.
> But look at her,
> She's covered
> A good third of the fence
> Her roots have thickened
> And she's started to bloom.

Students wore their red-yarn bracelets throughout the class. One of the students was taken out of school near the end of the class, as her mother had decided to move to a small town in Northern California. This student was reluctant to make this move, and was feeling very sad about leaving. She had some good friends in our program, so over the next year I used to ask about her and send greetings through her friends. A year later she came to visit one of these friends for a week, and she came to spend a few days at our school. When she came to my room she got a big hug, and with a great smile, she pulled back her sleeve to show me that her red-yarn bracelet was still tied around her left wrist.

It was shortly after this class that Angela approached me one day and said we needed to talk. "I haven't started my period yet," Angela said, "but when I do, I would like you to do a menstruation ritual for me. I have spoken to my parents about this and they think it's a great idea."

I am delighted and honored, and I tell her so. I ask her what she has in mind. "I will leave the ritual up to you," she says. "I don't want to have it until I have actually started menstruating. I want both my parents there, and some of my best friends, and I would like to invite Mr. Foreman."

Angela is a seventh grader when she makes this request. For the next few months her upcoming ritual is something to anticipate. When she returns from Winter break, Frank asks, "Is it time yet?"

No, Angela smiles, not yet.

Sometimes, after a weekend, Frank will say to her, "Now?"

No, Angela laughs, not yet.

I love watching her so comfortable and secure about her body, so sure of herself, so secure about our support, so ready to celebrate.

One day, Angela comes into my room during lunch. Frank and I are sitting at a table, eating. "NOW!" she beams. We jump up and give her a hug. We set a date for the ritual to take place at my house. Angela begins to use some of her time in her art class to make special invitations to this event.

Before I describe the ritual, I want to tell you about Angela in the sixth grade. It was clear right away that she would be one of our outstanding writers. But it is her heart that I remember, her willingness to share everything about herself in class. Angela's father is a gay man. Angela spent half her time in that family. I remember a photograph of her twelfth birthday party. Her father's partner had baked a wonderful, purple cake, and Angela brought a picture of herself with her father and her father's partner, happily grouped around this cake. She spent the other half of her time with her mother, her stepfather, and their two children, her half-brother and half-sister. During her sixth grade year, her mother and step-father divorced, and her mother became involved with another woman.

"You think you have problems," Angela said one day. "BOTH my parents are gay." But it was always clear that Angela loved both her parents, that they both loved her, and that while this was an adjustment for Angela, it was certainly not a tragedy. Her mother moved to Sonoma county, and Angela spent more time with her father.

That year we had the opportunity to enter a Bank of America essay contest. The assignment was to write about someone you admire, and Angela wrote a beautiful essay about her mother. As we read these essays in class, Angela shared that she wasn't sure whether or not to say anything about her mother's sexual identity. She wanted to, because that was a part of who her mother was. But she also wanted her essay to win, and she didn't think the Bank of America would award her for writing about a bisexual mother. She shared this dilemma with the class, and I remember that they took it seriously. In the end, she didn't say anything about her mother's sexual identification, but she felt bad about it. She won first prize.

On the morning of Angela's ritual, I went to the flower market. It was March, and I bought yellow tulips, purple irises, and white baby's breath. It was a time when I was between roommates, so I had a whole empty room available for this ritual. I put the flowers in vases, and began to collect symbols from around my house. On the floor I put a colorful, embroidered cloth from India, and a bright *khanga* (a brightly colored cloth worn by women) from Kenya. I placed two red candles, some incense, the Snake Goddess from Crete, a female Buddhasatva from India, a Masaii fertility doll from Kenya, some water from the Ganges River, a Greek bowl with ocean water, a seashell, and some stones on the altar. I added a small Pomo wedding basket, a Mexican angel candle, and a bottle of red wine. Now when I look back at the pictures, I see that there was a hearth broom in the room, although I didn't plan that.

Angela arrived with her mother and her mother's partner. Her father came alone. As Angela's friends arrived, I was touched by their attire — they wore hats, long gloves, and long skirts. I, too, had on a long dress. We sat in a circle, and I asked everyone to put something they had brought in the middle of the circle and to tell about it. Angela brought her grandmothers' photographs. Frank brought his grandfather's gold watch and some red Focaccia bread. The girls had brought flowers: narcissus, calla lilies, red tulips, and pink roses.

I told Frank and Angela's father that I had never done rituals with men before, and I didn't know how to do them with men, although I was really glad they were there and I wanted them to feel welcome. I explained that I would be conducting this ritual as if we were all women, so I asked them to get in touch with the female side of them for this ritual, or to pass when we went around the circle, whichever they felt most comfortable with.

Angela lit the candles, and we honored the East, the South, the West and the North, air, fire, water, and earth. We talked about menstruation as a gift of life. We passed a cup of wine around the circle, saying, "We are women who bleed but are not wounded. We bleed to bring life into the world."

We passed around a basket with beads in it. I asked everyone to take a bead, to hold it in her hand, and to think of it as a seed. As it warmed in the hand, to think of a gift that you want to give to Angela. Imagine that gift going into the bead/ seed. Then, we passed around a needle and thread. As each participant told Angela the gift they imagined for her, she would string the bead onto the thread. Angela received gifts like strength, humor, happiness. When it was my turn, I wished for her strong and healthy sexual ecstacy. "But not yet!" her father blurted out, and we all laughed. When the circle was complete, we gave Angela this beaded necklace, full of the love and best wishes of her friends and family.

Angela's mother read her a poem she had written for the occassion. This poem was a perfect closing for the ritual:

For Angela at Puberty[1]

I wish I had something
to pass on to you now —
a gold watch
a diamond ring —
something permanent and lasting.
But I have none of these
for you, never have had
such things as these
for you.
When I look back
at our lives together
I see the many homes
and people
we have shared
since your birth —
practically on the road.
And then I see in each place
with whomever we shared it
the comfort, warmth, security
of love.
I see many, many good times —
in country places
city flats
on the road.
All those birthday parties —
two a year for the first six
or so
in city parks and sandy beaches —

[1]Rogers, Lileth Lynn. "For Angela At Puberty," *Lileth Returns*. Garden Snake Press, Santa Barbara, 1989.

always lots of friends around.
In all the moves
the comings and goings of people
into and out of your life
I remember only once
(aside from the big move of your daddy)
when you were not ready.
You were four, and the landlord came
to our little house on Duncan Street
claiming for his own new place
the furniture his grandmother had left
years ago.
"Mommy!" you wailed.
"He's taking our refrigerator,
he's taking our couch!"
"It's okay, honey.
He thinks it's his stuff.
We'll get another fridge, another couch."
What am I passing on to you?
The impermanance of things—
their value only as tools
when we need them.
The changing landscape of where
and with whom
you live according to what's right
and best—or simply necessary—
at the time.
I pass on to you
flow.
This menstrual flow
we are celebrating today—
from woman to woman—

that I am—
that you are.
The beautiful, unique, miraculous
flow
of your Angela spirit.
Angela—felicitas—
Feliz Navidad.
Angela who, in her babyhood,
comforted all who held her.
Angela in her toddler self—
always coming back from
some nice old man on the street
with a hot quarter clutched tightly
in her fist.
(A casual blessing from a stranger.)
Angela as a little girl
dancing across the street to school
in a fairy costume or tap shoes!
Angela, the serious ballerina from age five onward
pudgy arms raised in grace
as she pirouetted around the living room—
whatever living room you found yourself in.
My Angela
Walt's Angela
Eliza and Noah's Angela
her many grandparents' Angela
her step-parents' Angela
her friends' and teachers' and roommates' Angela.
Angela who always flowed outward to us all.
Now today
I pass on to you
that this flow is good.

Better than good—
it's WONDERFUL!
It is your blessing
from me to me.
Thank you, daughter mine.

All of us were teary when Angela's mother finished her
poem. It was time to celebrate. We ate bread and cheese and
drank water and wine. The ritual became a party, and then
the other adults had to leave. The girls wanted to stay. "You
said you were going to do a guided fantasy," they said. "Yes, I
was, but the poem was so perfect it deserved to have the party
right afterwards," I said. The girls decide to stay and finish this
part, the other adults leave.

It is suddenly very cold in the room. I go to my bedroom to
find shawls for everyone. Rosie is retrieving her sweater from
my bed, and she looks sad. I ask her what is wrong. "I just had
my thirteenth birthday," she says. "I wish my mother had done
something like this for me."

I put my arm around her. "She would have, if she knew
about it," I tell her. "This ritual is really for all of us, Rosie. It
is specifically for Angela, but it is really about all of us. Don't
be hard on your mother for not thinking of this, women have
been taught for many many generations now, not to celebrate
their womanhood."

We return to the "ritual room" with warm shawls and sweaters, and everyone bundles up. I turn on the tape that will take
us on an internal journey. We make ourselves comfortable
and close our eyes. We go down a spiral staircase into deep
relaxation, until we enter a special room at the bottom of the
staircase. Behind a door someone is waiting for us. We open
the door, and greet the person waiting, who then gives us a gift

to bring back. In my case I meet my grandmother, who gives me her brown plastic rectangular hearing device, the one that the wires from her ears plugged into, the one she kept deep in her bosom, between her breasts. As a child, I used to climb on her slippery lap, and speak directly into her bosom, knowing that it was like speaking into her ear. Sometimes this hearing aid would cackle and crack with static.

The voice on the tape guides us back up the spiral staircase, until we open our eyes and re-enter the circle. Eve, sitting on my left, begins to cry. But it feels like a healthy, good cry, so I am not worried. I am glad the other adults are not there, however, as I think it would worry them. I put my arm around Eve's shoulders to comfort her. Let's go around the circle, and talk about what happened to us on this journey, I say. Eve, you can go last, or if you don't want to talk about what happened, you may pass.

The girls begin to tell their stories. I can't remember them all now, but I remember being astounded at how powerful they all were. One received a turquoise ring. One received a silver mirror. One received a white rose. One received a seashell. When we get to Eve, her crying has stopped, and she has been listening to the stories of the others. She tells us that she met her grandfather behind the door. This grandfather died just a few weeks ago. Eve didn't go to the hospital to see him before he died, and she feels bad about this. She is surprised to see him on this journey. His words to her are powerful. He tells her how much he loves her, how proud he is of her, how she should always remember that she comes from a strong and loving family, but that she should also always be herself, and listen to herself. He gives her a picture of himself as a young man.

When Eve tells us this story, she cries again. "Do you have this photograph of your grandfather in real life?" I ask. "Yes," she says. "I really have this picture. It is a real gift, not just a gift of my imagination." We are each touched by Eve's story. The ritual feels perfect.

The girls gather up their things before I drive them home. They thank me. If you want to give me a present, I say, write about this and give me a copy. While all of them intend to, only one of them does.

I describe the ritual to my friend Valorie. Each girl got a lovely, feminine gift, I say, except me. I tell her the story of my grandmother's brown plastic hearing aid, stuffed into her bosom. "Oh, Judy," she says. "You got that gift because you know how to listen with your heart."

This last Christmas Angela came over for dinner. She is a sophomore in college now, in Minnesota. We had a long conversation, catching up on news. She talked about her anger and fear when her father told her he was HIV positive. She talked about her pride in her mother. "I had to go to college to discover my mother as a scholar," she says. She talked about wanting to be a teacher, at least for a few years, and how distressed her father is about this decision. "It will look bad on your resume," he tells her.

"What kind of a teacher do you want to be?" I ask Angela.

"I want to do what you do," she says, and I think to myself, remember this moment.

7. Losing It: Notes About Field Trips

It is a beautiful, sunny, warm afternoon, perfect for driving across the Golden Gate Bridge. My friend Jeanne Gallo has taken her sixth-grade class on a two-day camping trip. She is camped at Kirby Cove, in the Golden Gate Headlands, a redwood grove right on the Pacific Ocean just west of the Golden Gate Bridge. My colleague Frank and I have been invited to join them for dinner, and as we drive over the bridge, I am relishing the fact that this is not *my* field trip. I have taken my students on this camping trip many times, and it feels luxurious to be driving over the bridge, rather than walking forty or fifty students across the bridge after having gotten up at five o'clock to load my car with two days worth of food, driving it across the bridge and parking it, and then meeting a friend to drive me back to school before eight. This time, it is Jeanne's turn. I get to just enjoy the company of the students, the view of the ocean, the smell of hot dogs on an open fire.

When we arrive the scene is peaceful. Students are lolling on the beach or playing volleyball or hiking in the hills. Jeanne is alone—the teacher with whom she planned this camping trip told her at the last minute that he had a class at state college that night, so he might as well just sleep at home. This leaves Jeanne alone with thirty students and no car in case of an emergency. Frank and I decide to stay until bedtime, in case any students need a ride. (I have taken many sick children home over the years, and I've visited the emergency room more than once — I know that a car is essential.)

While the students are having a good time, Jeanne and Frank and I sit at a picnic table in the sun and begin to tell field trip stories. I strongly believe in taking children out of the classroom and over the years I have taken many field trips. Almost always, something has gone wrong. I tell about the time when I was a very young teacher and I believed my students from Hunter's Point would benefit from a day spent at San Francisco State College. I arranged for the Black Students' Union to give them a guided tour. On the way home, however, my students set fire to the back seat of the bus. The bus driver pulled over to the side of the road and yelled at me, "Lady, can't you control those kids?"

I did the only thing I could think of doing. I put my hand on my hip, mustered what dignity I could, and replied, "Does it look like I can control these kids?"

He put us off the bus. I took this same class to visit the *Sun Reporter,* the only black-owned-and-run newspaper in San Francisco. While waiting at a bus stop to transfer, a candy truck pulled up in front of a drugstore and the driver *left its back door up while he delivered several boxes of candy inside*! My students saw this as an open invitation, and I became octopus-like, using my arms, legs, head, and body to block grabs for Hersheys, Snickers, Reese's Peanut Butter Cups, Milky Ways and Oh Henrys. It was about this time that I began wearing disguises on field trips: dark glasses, hats, bulky coats.

Then there was the time I had to write a note home explaining why one of my students had whiskey sloshed all over his sweatshirt. We were on a crowded bus, and when it lurched to one side, a drunk man — trying to drink out of a bottle in a paper bag—missed, and the contents spilled into my student's sweatshirt hood. "Please excuse the smell in Jimmy's sweatshirt . . ."

Or the time that Kathie and I were walking sixty students to the streetcar stop after an afternoon of ice-skating. When I rounded the corner, sixty students were running around in circles, laughing, covering their eyes, totally confused. It was as if the God Pan himself had appeared among them. It took a moment to figure out what was going on, but I soon saw that across the street in a second-floor motel picture window, a very fat naked man was waving a bottle of spirits, laughing, and moving his hips so that his penis flopped back and forth. I walked calmly into the motel office to report this offense, and asked the proprietor to call the police. When the man saw me heading towards the office, he closed the drapes.

On another occasion I was walking a sixth grade class to the bus stop after attending a play at University High School. These students also suddenly started running around, screaming, and laughing, this time because of two dogs mating. For those of you who are not teachers, or for those of you who do not teach sixth grade, believe me, you have not lived until you walk thirty-six sixth graders past two mating dogs.

While Jeanne and Frank and I are visiting, her students organize and cook dinner, serving us at our picnic table. I tell Jeanne about the time we reserved this campground only to discover once we were here that the other part of it had been reserved by a B-movie company. For a film about a war between Arabs and Africans, they were shooting a night scene in which the Arabs landed on the beach and the Africans defended it. The beach, the hills, and the bunkers were wired with fake explosives. Those and the strong lights kept everyone up all night. The only good thing was that a baseball hero who was starring in the movie came and had hot dogs with the kids.

Fortunately for me, this was someone else's field trip. I just visited to give moral support, and got to drive home and sleep in my own bed, and heard the horror stories later.

I tell about the time that I had forty students walking to the theater from the bus stop, when three strangers singled out one of my male students and practiced kung fu on him and then ran away. And the time I arranged to spend a whole day at the zoo with some other teachers and our classes, but we were sent home by the police when some students broke all the phones to steal change. Or the time I took eighth graders on a bus to Sacramento, stopping at the Milk Farm for a meal on the way home. It wasn't until the Milk Farm sent a large bill to my school that I realized that the students had helped themselves to the large stack of milk chocolate bars displayed by the cash register.

On a recent trip to the Oakland Museum to see a display of African American quilts, several students got lost. Two parents had come along to help, and we boarded two different subway cars. About six girls who were in the car next to mine decided to take advantage of my not being there, and began walking from one car to the other, which they are not supposed to do. When we came to our stop, they didn't know it was time to get off since they were in a different car. As I was counting noses in the station, I saw the six of them pressed up against the glass in the last car, looking worried and distraught as the train pulled out.

The rest of the kids were very upset. "What will happen to them? What should they do? Will they get in trouble?" I calmed them down. "You wait here," I told them. "The girls will have sense enough to get off at the next station and come back. I'll go upstairs and speak to the station master." I did so, and explained the problem. She was kind enough to phone ahead to the next station and ask the security people to meet my students and make sure they returned by the next train. I rejoined the class, confident that the girls would show up soon. But several trains later I began to worry. I revisited the stationmaster, and she phoned ahead to check with security. They reported that the girls had not disembarked. So she got on the paging system and started to announce, "Will Ms. Logan's students please call 214. Will Ms. Logan's students please call 214." I returned to the station downstairs to see the rest of my class running around wildly looking for a phone.

"Not you," I explained. "We want the *lost* students to call."

Shortly thereafter a train arrived with the lost girls. I was relieved as I had begun to really worry. So had they. Two of them were crying and needed to be held, the other four were clearly shaken. We all sat down in a quiet place to hear what had happened.

The girls explained. Realizing they had missed our stop, the girls traveled through the double door again, only this time to the front of the car until they reached the conductor and told him their plight. He advised them to wait two stops before getting off, as the next station had a complicated way of trying to return, whereas the second station was quite simple. They stayed together and followed his advice, but it took a while as the second station was quite far away. I asked them what they had learned from this experience, and they came up with all the right answers ("Stay with the group, stay together"). I complimented them on making good decisions and reassured them that they were now fine.

Jeanne's class is building a campfire and getting ready for entertainment. It continues to be the perfect field trip. I tell Jeanne my two favorite field trip stories.

I allowed a few sixth graders to accompany a Shakespeare class to an outdoor performance of *Macbeth*. My seventh and eighth grade class had read and studied the play, but the sixth graders had not. They were eager to go however, and they were good students, so I let them. The performance was terrible—one of the worst I have ever seen. Returning from the theater, one sixth grader walked beside me in silence. I could feel her puzzling things out. Finally she said, "Which one was Macbeth?"

Another time, I had taken a large group of students to see a matinee performance of Chekov's *The Cherry Orchard*. The performance was magnificent, and the students were moved. One particularly sensitive sixth grader walked beside me silently for some time, and again, I could feel her puzzling things out. "That was so sad," she said.

"Yes," I reply.

"I mean it was *really* sad," she said again. "Sadder than E.T."

So she chose Anton Chekov over Steven Speilburg. Who says field trips aren't worth it?

Back at the campgrounds, it is night and nobody is sick, nobody is homesick, nobody is misbehaving. Frank and I can leave Jeanne and her class to sleep out under the stars, with the sound of the ocean in their ears. We congratulate her again on having arranged the perfect field trip, hug her goodbye, and begin the slow winding drive up the dirt road to the top of the hill. When we get to the top, a ranger's truck pulls over and stops us. "Are you with the school group camped out below?" they ask us.

"Unofficially we are, officers. Why, is there a problem?"

"Yes, Ma'am, there is a problem. We have to get those kids out of there right away. There's just been a big earthquake in Alaska and there's a tsunami heading this way. We may have twenty-foot tidal waves. We have orders to clear all coastal areas. I want those kids on high ground in fifteen minutes. Tell them to leave their food, sleeping bags and other equipment behind, and to just hike immediately to high ground."

Frank drives down to tell Jeanne and the kids. I hike to a pay phone by the bridge to call the principal and ask him to call teachers to volunteer to drive the kids home. It is two hours before everyone is safely delivered home. The tsunami never comes. So much for the perfect field trip.

8. Walking in Someone Else's Shoes

Just what is a multicultural and gender-inclusive curriculum? Each year I learn something new about it. While I am uncomfortable with isolating February as Black History Month, or March as Women's History Month, I find that such things do provide me with community support for particular projects. For example, my class researches and writes essays on women from history in order to participate in the NOW essay contest. Because these essays have to be submitted in mid-December, however—even though the reception for the winners doesn't take place until Women's History Month—we begin working on them in the fall and thus their focus covers more than half the year.

In February I especially focus on Black History. I have asked students to choose one African American person, to research his or her life completely, and to come to class as that person in order to tell the story of his or her life. Students are encouraged to use photographs, illustrations, costumes, props, music, drama and videotapes in order to make their subject's life real to the class. I provide a list of suggestions to which students can add. Last year I noticed that while two girls chose to be males (Gordon Parks and Martin Luther King), none of the males chose to be females. I began to wonder what I could do to help all students feel comfortable exploring both male and female lives. One year I modified my usual Black History Month assignment so that each student was required to do two reports—one on a male, and one on a female.

Initially, I was surprised that not one student objected to doing two reports, or to "becoming" a person of the opposite gender. All of their questions were about whether or not they could extend my list. By this time in the semester they knew that I like them to collaborate and alter my assignments. But as they raised their hands to ask if they could be Janet Jackson or Bill Cosby, I realized that they saw this assignment as an opportunity to become one of their heroes from the sports or entertainment field. Instead of saying no, I said yes to each request and listed each name on the board. Then I asked them to look at the list of names. We had only athletes and entertainers. "This is a great list," I said, "but it is not black history. In fact, I would be embarrassed to have this list leave the room as our concept of black history, because, even though these great people are an integral part of black history, they are not the whole picture. How would you feel if I said we were going to study white history and then we only studied movie stars and sports heroes? I know that you don't know yet about the people I put on the list, but trust me, they have interesting lives, and you will like getting to know them." Slowly hands were raised and students began trading their heroes for names unknown. By not saying no to them in the first place, we as a class were allowed to confront our limited perceptions of black contributions to society.

Once I had accomplished the selection process, my job as teacher for the next several weeks was to bring a lot of material to class. We watched the PBS series on *Getting to Know Me*, ten half-hour dramatic programs on a black family, each of which celebrates some aspect of black culture. We watched segments of programs on Black History. We read poems, listened to music, and read stories. Each day I would say, "Class, who in this class is Alice Walker?" Pauline would raise her hand. "Pauline, you wrote the poems I will be reading today." And Pauline would smile. Or, "Who in this class is Malcolm X?" David would raise his hand. "David, you will be making a very important speech in today's video, watch carefully." And he would. Or, "Who is Bernice Johnson Reagan? Keishon, you wrote this music, and you will see yourself in this tape." Of course, I also provided them with library time so they could research independently.

The last week of February I get to sit in the back of the room and watch some amazing presentations. Some students choose to do both their male and female roles in succession; some do just one, then wait until later for their second presentation. Their work delights me. Celeste comes in one morning before homeroom and hands me a white florist's box, and asks me to keep it in the refrigerator for her. Later in class, she carefully, tenderly pins a white gardenia in her hair before beginning her report as Billie Holiday. Her friend pushes the on and off button on the tape recorder so that Billie's music is part of her report.

Bret, whose usual attire is jeans and a sports-logo tee shirt, comes to school in a black suit, dons black horned-rimmed glasses, and becomes Langston Hughes. Afterwards, he disappears behind the file cabinets, and a few minutes later reappears as Sojourner Truth, wearing a large housedress and a cotton scarf on his head. Akiko, her long, black hair pulled back in a pony tail to keep it off her face, has taken a large poster board and cut a hole out of the center, just large enough to stick her face through. Around this hole she has drawn hair, and a small-scale but muscular body in boxing trunks, with gloves on, in a ring. She tells her story as Muhammad Ali. Then, she turns the poster board around and pokes her face through again. On this side she has drawn an elaborate hairdo, a shimmering gown. She holds a microphone as she stands on stage, and she tells us her story as Tina Turner. Paul Robeson shows us a part of a film he made, and we listen to him sing. Jesse Jackson and Shirley Chisholm give their campaign speeches. Mary McLeod Bethune tells us about her struggles to begin her school, and Sara Lawrence Lightfoot shares her educational philosophies. Students refer to 3x5 cards, but for the most part they have internalized their stories and tell them from memory.

Celeste, this time as Joe Louis, wears a purple silk robe on the back of which she has taped the words, BROWN POWER. When she gets to the moment in her story when she is fighting for the heavyweight championship of the world, she says, "But wait, it was such an exciting moment, I can't possibly describe it to you. Let me show you . . . " and she slips a tape into the video machine.

Pauline climbs up on my tall stool. She wraps herself in a large purple shawl. "Dear God," she begins. "My name is Alice Walker . . . "

Sometimes I interview the students while they are in character. "So, James Meredith, there you were with all those TV cameras, national guardsmen, hostile crowds. How did you feel as you walked down that street toward school?" The students reply in character. "I was scared, but I was determined. And I felt proud. I knew what I was doing was dangerous, but I knew I needed that education and I wasn't going to let anything stop me. I had a lot of support from my friends and community." Sometimes a student will say something like, "Well, Ms. Logan, this happened a long time ago, and I can't remember right now how I felt, but I'll look at my journals tonight and give it some thought, and get back to you tomorrow."

A nice moment in this assignment: Lena, as Zora Neale Hurston, to Bret, as Langston Hughes, "Bret, I know you!" And she tells us about how Zora and Langston's lives intersected. Other students begin telling how they knew or admired other students' characters. They say things like, "I found you in my life too!" We have moved from individual presentations to an exploration of how these people were related in time and space.

Many weeks later the class is on a field trip to the Oakland Museum to see a show called, "Strength and Diversity: A History of the Japanese American Woman." Some parents have volunteered to accompany us, and as we walk towards the museum, Bret's mother says, "Judy, I want to tell you how much I appreciate your social studies program. Not long ago, Bret had some friends over from another school, and I overheard them talking about their classes. Bret had a wealth of information about women and about minorities. And his friends didn't know anything about the people he was talking about. I'm really grateful that he has your class." Nothing is sweeter to a teacher than praise and appreciation from parents.

9. From Mother Jones to Shoshannah's Mom

It is 1986 and I see a flier telling me that the San Francisco branch of the National Organization of Women is sponsoring an essay contest in middle schools for Women's History Month. The essay must be about a famous woman in history and it must be thoroughly researched and well-written. The text is to be submitted on one side of the paper only, with the names of the writer, the school, and the teacher on the back of each page, so that the essay will be anonymous as they are being judged. My students have done a lot of work on women in history, so we decide to enter. Each sixth grader writes an essay as part of a class assignment. I announce the contest to my seventh and eighth graders, and some of them choose to enter as well. Essay prizes are $75, $50, and $25 for first, second and third place; ribbons and certificates will also be awarded.

We read each other's essays and decide as a class which ones to submit. We are supposed to turn in the "top three" from each class, but since I have these students for three periods a day for three subjects, we turn in nine essays to represent us.

Some time later I receive a phone call telling me that we have won first and second place for sixth grade, second place for seventh grade, and an honorable mention. Hallie has won for writing about Mother Jones, Emma for Laura Ingalls Wilder, Vanessa for Virginia Woolf, and Maria for Alice Walker. I have a great time phoning the students, putting their names in the daily school bulletin, announcing the results in class, and later attending a reception sponsored by NOW at which each winner reads her essay aloud and receives her awards. Some days later I receive a note from Hallie's mother: "Three winners in one class? You're the one who deserves the prize. What you have done for both my kids' writing is a gift I'll never forget." I still have this note on my dresser.

One day Maria comes to class and tells me she has attended the graduation ceremonies at her elementary school. "And guess who was there," she tells me. "Alice Walker!" I am delighted as Maria describes how she went up and introduced herself to Alice Walker as someone who had recently won an essay contest by writing about her.

The next year I announce to the sixth graders that we will again be entering the contest. "I expect some of you will win this year," I say. They become anxious and angry. "How unfair! What if we don't win? This is too much pressure," and so on. "Oh, it's okay if you don't win," I say, "but ever since I have been teaching sixth grade I have entered my students' writing in some essay contest or another, and we have always had a winner. This class is full of fine writers. It's okay if we don't win this year, but I will be surprised if we don't. Anyway, the contest is a long way off. We will learn a lot about writing between now and then."

Again, the NOW contest is a mandatory assignment for sixth graders, an optional one for seventh and eighth graders. Again, I am delighted to receive a phone call telling me that Hallie has won first place for her seventh grade essay on Sarah Winnemucca; Janet second place for her sixth grade essay on Helen Keller; and Amelia seventh grade second place for Clara Barton. There are also two honorable mentions: Skye for her essay on Winnie Mandela, and Noah for his essay on his grandmother, Ruth Asawa. I am delighted to have our first male winner and the first essay about a family member, his grandmother. Again we attend the reception. I ask Hallie what she will do with her $75. "It is my sister Rosie's birthday this month," she says, "and I am going to donate it to the Nicaraguan Ambulance Fund in her name."

The next year I give my we-have-always-won-a-contest speech. Again the students become angry and accuse me of being unfair. Again I reassure them that it is okay if we don't win. In doing this, I not only challenge them, but also deflect onto the past classes the competition that they might feel with each other. This way, if only one person wins, that person is winning for the whole class and places the class in the we-have-always-won-a-contest hall of fame. But not just one person wins the contest. This year the phone call tells me we have won first place in sixth-, seventh-, and eighth grade categories; second place for the sixth and seventh grades; third place for the sixth and seventh grades; and we have five honorable mentions. "Isn't anyone else entering the contest?" I ask meekly. "Oh yes," the caller assures me, "we had more entries than ever this year. Almost all middle schools in the city are participating, as well as some private schools."

The students are thrilled when I make the announcement. This year they have written about Margaret Sanger, Emma Goldman, Winnie Mandela, Dian Fossey, Hildegarde of Bingen, Anne Frank, Jane Addams, Lucretia Mott, and Joan Baez. Hallie, as an eighth grader, has won first place again for an essay on Mother Teresa. This year she hadn't wanted to write an essay, which is optional for eighth graders. She is very busy and I think she is a little embarrassed that she won first place two years in a row. By this time, Hallie and I are good friends, and I feel comfortable pushing her a little, and she takes it well. I pop a video on Mother Teresa into the VCR for her to watch. "You'll do better with a rough draft than most people would with hours of work," I tell her. "It would be a shame not to enter this year when you have done so well in the past."

I am particularly happy with her first prize award. So are the NOW people. At the reception they call Hallie up specially, and give her flowers. They also call me up specially, and give me flowers. I say a few words thanking them for this opportunity to write about women and predict that some day we will be writing about Hallie.

The NOW group also asks me to come to their meeting and talk about feminist curriculum, since I must be doing something right in order to have all these kids writing winning essays. I have a good time speaking to their group. They meet in the Women's Building on 18th Street, which used to be Dovre Hall, the Norwegian Club. As the grandchild of Norwegian immigrants, I spent a lot of time there at Christmas parties, weddings, and family reunions. The room where NOW meets, where I stand and talk about my classes, is the room where my parents held their wedding reception and where my grandparents had their Golden Anniversary party.

For my presentation I bring in some of my students' work, I show slides of their work, and I talk about Peggy McIntosh's Phase Theory. The NOW group decides to change its policy and allow students to write about non-famous people in history, like mothers and grandmother

The next year we again win first place for sixth, seventh and eighth grades, second place for sixth, seventh, and eighth grades, and third place for sixth and seventh grades. Once more, we have five honorable mentions. Even I'm impressed. Students have written about family, friends and teachers, as well as Cyndi Lauper, Joan Baez, Rosa Parks, Shirley Chisholm, Benazir Bhutto, and Dianne Feinstein, the mayor of San Francisco.

Ben has written a wonderful essay about his mother, who is a midwife, and his essay includes a summary of the history of midwifery. At the reception, he asks his mother to stand while he reads it aloud, and we all have a teary moment. Thea has written about Mayor Feinstein. She sends a copy of her essay to the mayor's office. Later she receives a beautiful crystal vase from Feinstein, and she is able to meet her in person at a reception on Treasure Island.

In 1990 I give my we-have-always-won-a-contest speech to my new sixth graders. Students gulp and protest as usual, and I give my same calm, reassuring, it's-okay-if-we-don't-but-I'll-be-surprised reply. Again we win first place for sixth, seventh, and eighth grades. We win second place in sixth, seventh, and eighth grades. We win third place for sixth and seventh grades, and we get four honorable mentions. "Are you sure other people are entering this contest?" I ask my NOW friends. They tell me they had over 500 entries this year. My students have written about Elizabeth Gurley Flynn, Sylvia Plath, Michelle Cliff, Helen Caldicott, and Simone de Beauvoir, as well as aunts, teachers, mothers and grandmothers. Two of their essays are published in a San Francisco newspaper.

Rain has graduated from eighth grade and is a freshman in high school. Her mother sends me a note telling me that Rain just won an essay contest on Martin Luther King, and she is kind enough to send me a copy of the essay and a program from the awards ceremony along with the note. Rain entered this contest on her own, she tells me.

Last year as a sixth grader Shoshannah wrote her essay on Ann Richards, who spoke at the Democratic convention. She didn't win a prize although it was a great essay. Some family friends, who have a business greeting and escorting visiting dignitaries around San Francisco, remembered Shoshannah's essay and invited her to accompany them when Ann Richards came to the city for a book-signing party. Shoshannah asked me for a copy of her essay. She met Ann Richards and they had their picture taken together as Shoshanah gave her this copy. The next year Shoshannah was invited to the Inaugural Ball in Texas when Ann Richards became governor. I remember that Shoshannah wrote a wonderful piece in the sixth grade about her three heroes. They were Hallie, her classmate, Judy Logan, her teacher, and Ann Richards. I am thrilled that she got to meet her third hero.

This year Shoshannah wins first place for her seventh grade essay on Janet Stafford, a neighbor, family friend, and pediatrician who is a wife and mother in an interracial marriage. In this essay she focuses on Janet's courageous battle with breast cancer, celebrates her survival instincts, and describes how the battle with cancer helped Janet to see the children under her care at the hospital as survivors. When Shoshannah finishes reading her essay, she introduces Janet to the audience. It is another teary moment. After the NOW reception Shoshannah's mother takes Janet, Shoshannah and me to lunch. I learn that Janet was present at Shoshannah's birth.

Later that year Shoshannah's mother, Judith, discovers a lump in her breast. She calls me to tell me what is going on, when she is going for her biopsy, and how she is feeling. Shoshannah comes in to see me one morning before school. "It was malignant," she says. "Oh shit," I blurt out, without thinking. When I call Judith later, she says Shoshannah came home and said, "Mom, Ms. Logan never swears, but today when I told her she said 'Oh shit.'" We talk about her upcoming surgery, her chemotherapy, her radiation. I try to keep in close touch but Shoshannah seems calm and doesn't want to talk about it much. However, she begins writing for the writing club about incredibly angry daughters and dying mothers.

The next year I am going on sabbatical leave. "But what about the NOW essay contest?" the students ask. "Mr. Foreman will do the essay contest next year," I tell them. "If there is a winner from our school, I promise I will come home from wherever I am to attend the reception in March." When it is time for the contest, Frank puts a tremendous amount of energy into helping students choose topics, selecting the essays, and submitting them. In February he proudly calls me to tell me that our students have won first place in seventh and eighth grades, second place in seventh and eighth grades, third place in sixth and eighth grades, and four honorable mentions. I am thrilled; the students are thrilled. When it is time for the reception my friend Nancy Letts is presenting at a conference in San Francisco, and she takes time to attend with me. This year students have written about Eleanor Roosevelt, Indira Gandhi, Amelia Earhart, Georgia O'Keeffe, Mary McLeod Bethune, Imogen Cunningham, and Morgain le Fay, as well as about parents, teachers, and grandmothers. But it is Shoshannah's essay on her mother that touches me most deeply. She titles it "A Will To Live," and it is a beautiful essay about her mother's life, including this last year's successful struggle with cancer. Nancy sits on one side of me and Frank sits on the other side of me and we all three quietly cry through the whole presentation.

This year in September when I return to teaching, I will say to my sixth graders, "Ever since I started teaching sixth grade we have had city-wide essay contest winners in this class. My classes have a reputation for winning contests." And the students will say, "That's really unfair to put that kind of pressure on us. How will we feel if we don't win a contest?" And I will say, "Oh, it's okay with me if we don't win, I don't expect this to go on forever. But I will be surprised if we don't, because we have such good writers in this class . . . "

Who knows what will happen?

10. Kerry

Some of Kerry's story I have already told, or alluded to in Chapter 4. Here is the rest of what I remember. As a sixth grader, Kerry was shy and withdrawn. She was pale, with long pale blond hair, and though she was a talented writer, she didn't speak in class easily. Her only friend in class was Tasha, who had serious problems. Tasha lived with her father and her two-year-old sister. Her father was dying of AIDS, suffering from dementia, and was sometimes violent. I remember that she was not allowed to come to my house for a tea party or to attend field trips that extended past three o'clock. She was in charge of her little sister whenever she was not in school, and I remember her telling me that when her father ranted and raved, she would lock herself in her bedroom with her little sister on her lap, and play video games as loud as she could, to keep from being scared. We had counselors and social workers on this case, and Tasha's father died before they could remove her from the home. She then left the school and moved to another city in order to live with her mother. While she was at our school however, she and Kerry ate lunch together, and took the bus to and from school together. Except for Tasha, Kerry was a loner.

After Tasha left, Kerry bonded with my student teacher, Ellen, and wrote in her journal one day, "Would you like to have dinner together sometime? We could go for sushi." Kerry was lonely. In October, for our Spooky Tales Contest, she wrote a story called "The Glass Doll and The Music Box" (see the end of this chapter), about a girl who kills her mother and father. By this time I was worried about her, and after talking to her school counselor, we met with her father and suggested some professional counseling. Kerry had lived alone with her father since she was seven. We set up a session at Kaiser Permanente Hospital, but I found out later that they didn't attend. We also saw to it that a counselor intern met with Kerry regularly in school.

I spent that summer in Ireland. I returned in the fall and gave Kerry photographs of the Kerry Theater, the Kerry Market, the Kerry bus, and Kerry street signs.

In the seventh grade she began to be absent frequently, and for long stretches. We called home about it and her father said she was suffering from cramps and headaches, but he would try to get her to school more regularly. Her appearance began to change. She dyed her hair a flat black and shaved part of her head. Sometimes parts of her hair were purple. She had lots of earrings in one ear and wore only black clothes. But she had more friends and she continued to do well in her classes.

In the eighth grade her appearance became more extreme. It seemed that her hair changed every week. Sometimes the pale blond hair just ended in black or purple, as her real hair grew out. But the more bizarre her appearance, the more I saw the pale sixth grader underneath. The day after Halloween, she comes to my class looking really terrible. "What happened?" I ask. "I've been out all night long, riding the buses," she says. "I'm afraid to go home, I had a fight with my father, I'm exhausted, I'm scared." "Are you on any drugs?" "No."

She really looks awful, like she could collapse. She lies down on the classroom couch, I put my coat over her, and she sleeps deeply for hours. I call my friend, Nancy, who is a health worker, and who has counseled Kerry before. "I think she is in a serious crisis," I say, and Nancy kindly agrees to come to school and to meet with her the next day. I offer to call Kerry's father for her and to mediate their meeting, but Kerry declines, and promises to go home. We talk about alternatives to riding the buses all night in case she feels she has to leave again. She knows about Huckleberry House, the refuge for teenage runaways.

The next day, Nancy meets with her for some time. "She is in a crisis," she says, "but she's handling it. She knows her alternatives; she is really very mature."

One day, a group of students stay in during lunch and they are sitting on the floor visiting together while I am puttering around. They are in a heated discussion about something or other. Later, I ask one of them, "What's up?"

"Kerry's steady boyfriend was at a party with someone else on Halloween. Kerry wasn't there. He made out with the other girl at the party. Some people think that we should tell Kerry, some people think it is not our business to tell her." "Hmmm. That's a dilemma all right."

Someone does tell her, eventually, and she does break off this steady relationship. Everyone likes Kerry, and she gets a lot of support from her many friends.

But the Monday before Thanksgiving, during homeroom, a student comes to tell me that Kerry has just been found in a remote corner of the third floor. She brought a razor blade and her baby blanket to school, and had gone outside on a terrace and slit her wrists. She has been taken to the principal's office, and is waiting for an ambulance. I start to tremble. Because this is the worst thing that can happen to a student under her care, this is the worst thing that can happen to a teacher, I think. No, the worst thing would be if her attempt were successful. I don't have a class, so I go to tell Frank. "I will go see her," I tell him, "then I will come and cover your class so you can go see her."

When I enter the office, she is huddled by the desk, her wrists wrapped up. Her counselor is there with her. I go put my hand on her shoulder, but she shrugs it off and says angrily, "This was *not* supposed to happen." "What *was* supposed to happen?" I ask. "I was supposed to die," she says.

"I'm glad you didn't die, Kerry," I say. "Your counselor will go with you to the hospital. I will call you later. I am going to watch Mr. Foreman's class so he can come and see you before you go. You'll be well taken care of."

As I walk to Frank's class, I meet students from our program who are in the hall, scared and horrified at what has happened. The news is traveling fast. When Frank returns from seeing Kerry, we agree to call Suicide Prevention and to get counselors into the school immediately. First, I go upstairs to see Suzanne, our audio visual clerk, who found Kerry and took her razor blade away. Suzanne lost her younger sister to suicide so I know this must be a particularly bad experience for her. I give her a hug, I thank her for what she did, I tell her that Kerry is on her way to the hospital, and that the counselor will stay with her and make sure she gets admitted for treatment. "I was glad I could help save her," Suzanne says, and her mouth is trembling. I wonder if my mouth is trembling too.

I call Nancy, the counselor who already met with Kerry, and she comes to school immediately and helps me make phone calls. Suicide Prevention agrees to send counselors to meet with the seventh-and-eighth grade classes in the afternoon. I call McAteer High School, and they agree to send students from their peer counseling center immediately. Students are clustering in my classroom, crying, holding on to each other, talking. "Kerry is going to be okay," I reassure them, "but what has happened is really terrible—it is okay to be scared, sad, whatever." By noon, Margo has arrived from suicide prevention. She's a former model now turned counselor, and her tall, calm, grounded presence helps us all. We decide to put two classes together for sixth and seventh period. Nancy will meet with one group, Margo with the other one. We want to send a letter home to parents, telling them what happened, so that they can talk to their children and help them cope, but the administration doesn't think it's a good idea. (Two days later, however, they give their approval and we send a letter home.)

Margo goes around the room and has everyone tell how she or he is feeling. There is a lot of guilt, anger, fear, and sorrow: "If only I had known, I could have done something." "I said something mean to her last week, could that have made her do this?" "I just feel really afraid." "What if she were really dead now?" We talk about how suicide is a permanent solution to a temporary problem. We talk about how to get help if someone threatens suicide.

Margo also meets with the teachers. "You are doing the right thing," she says, "Just let them keep talking about their feelings. Watch for students who seem isolated. Suicide attempts affect everyone involved, and people in the school are at risk for at least six months—teachers included—even students from other programs who did not know Kerry. We can expect other suicide gestures, we should be on the alert for signs, and we should take all symptoms seriously." It feels like the earthquake experience of 1989. We are under stress, preparing for possible aftershocks.

On the outside I am calm and professional. On the inside I am like a fierce tiger. I cannot do anything for Kerry right now—she has been admitted to a hospital for psychiatric treatment for at least a month — but I can be alert and watchful so that this doesn't happen to any of the others. I know that suicide gestures in teenagers can spread like a bad rash. I am terrified that someone else will try this and succeed. At night when I go to bed, I mentally go over the day, checking to see if there was any behavior that I should be noticing. The tiger in me prowls and paces, ever watchful.

We arrange for a suicide prevention counselor to address the faculty so that all teachers can get information on what to watch for, on what to do. We arrange for an evening parent meeting so that Margo can help parents deal with their feelings, and so that she can educate them about suicide. We encourage all students to talk to their parents. We arrange for the peer counselors to be in my classroom for the next two days. If only I can make it until Thanksgiving, I think, I will have four days to rest and recover.

The first suicide gesture comes just one day after Kerry's attempt, on the Tuesday before Thanksgiving. The counseling office calls me. "We have Matt in the office," they say. "We have taken a razor blade away from him. He has cut himself up and down his arms. Although he is not your student, he says he won't speak to anyone but you and Frank."

I get Frank and we go to the office. On the way, I think about Matt. I don't really know him well — I know he is friends with a lot of my students, especially Kerry, and he comes into my room to visit sometimes, but I have never had him as a student. He is a slight, quick, thin child with a stray puppy look.

When I get to the office he is sitting in a chair looking at the floor. "Let me see your arms," I ask, and he pushes up his sleeves. My heart breaks when I see the thirty or so superficial slashes on his arms. What is this about? I ask myself. Why did he want to see me and Frank?

I lean down so my eyes are even with his. "Matt, did you do this so we would send you to the hospital with Kerry, so that you can be with her?"

He starts to cry. "Yes," he says. "She needs to be with her friends. She shouldn't be all alone."

"She isn't all alone," I say, "she is in good hands, and people will take good care of her." I look at the counselor. "I think we should call the hospital and let him talk to her," I say. "He needs to hear that she is okay." She nods and dials the phone. Frank and I stay with him until Matt's mother arrives to take him to a therapist.

Parents call me and they too are upset. Johannes' mother arranges to take a whole carload of kids down to the hospital to see Kerry. "I know it's too soon for them to visit with her," she says, "but they need to see her, even if it's just down the hall. I need to see her," she says. She starts to cry. "This is so sad. When she gets out, she could come to our house and stay with us," she says.

It feels like I am always on the phone. When I am not on the phone, the tiger in me is prowling around, observing student behavior. If a child lingers at the pencil sharpener too long, I begin a mental file on him. We make it to Thanksgiving.

But on a crowded streetcar on the day before Christmas vacation, as we return from taking too many kids to see *A Christmas Carol*, Frank tells me, "Frankie says that James is talking about suicide. We better take him into school and talk to him when we get back." James? He is one of our best students. He has a great family. His mother is a professor, his father is has a catering business. Both parents come to all school meetings. Both parents are clearly involved with and concerned about their children's lives. Why would James be thinking of suicide? But we take him up to my room when we get back to school. It is four or five o'clock and everyone else goes home.

"Are you thinking of committing suicide, James?"

"Yes."

"Have you thought about how you would do it?"

"No."

"Have you thought about when you would do it?"

"No. I don't want you to tell anyone about this," he says.

"Why are you thinking about it?" we ask.

"I'm just not getting along with my parents," he says vaguely. "I like Frankie, but she doesn't like me."

Frank talks to him about adolescent problems, about suicide being a permanent solution to a temporary problem, about talking to his parents. We negotiate a contract with him. He will not do anything without calling us first. When he leaves, we talk about this, but neither of us can figure out why he is suddenly in crisis.

It is the first day of Christmas vacation, but I am awake, tossing and turning all night. Something is wrong, something is wrong, something is wrong. If I go over everything carefully enough, there is a clue somewhere as to what is really wrong with James. I think about it all day Saturday, as I go about my life, but I remain deeply puzzled. Something just doesn't make sense. I toss and turn again on Saturday night. What is it? What is it? Finally, about four in the morning, I sit up in bed. My brain finally offers up some information. It was James who told Kerry that her boyfriend had been making out with someone else at the Halloween party. I also remember that James was not in school the week of Thanksgiving—he flew to New York to visit his grandparents for the holiday. He missed all of the counseling sessions. As soon as I have figured this out, I go to sleep.

The next morning I call James' home early. His mother answers the phone. "There is a serious problem I would like to come and talk to you about," I say.

"Good," she says, "I wish someone would come and tell me what's going on. Our phone is ringing off the hook with James' friends, and he won't talk to us."

"I'll be right over," I say.

When I get there, she makes coffee, and James and his mother and father and I sit around the kitchen table. I have asked him to join us so he can hear everything I say. "I know you asked me not to talk about this, I tell him, but this is too serious for me to keep to myself." I tell about his suicide threat, about Kerry's history, and about how I finally figured out the connection between his story and Kerry's story. "He needs counseling right away," I say. His mother is very supportive. His father is polite but defensive, and I don't blame him. Here I am in his home on a Sunday morning describing a serious problem. If Frank and I were so surprised, imagine how James' parents must feel. When I finish my story, I look at James. He seems more relieved than angry at me, he says that everything I have said is true, he feels responsible for Kerry's suicide attempt. His parents promise to get immediate help, and I take my leave.

A big voice inside of me says, *Take care of yourself. Go get some breakfast. Go home and go to bed.* I take a bath, as I have that sticky film all over that comes with emotional tension. That night, James' father calls me. "I want to thank you for coming over this morning," he says. "We had a long talk with James after you left. But, he was wrong. He shouldn't have told Kerry anything about her boyfriend. I think he understands that."

"I don't think this is about making a judgment," I say. "This is about giving him some love and support. He's feeling guilty and vulnerable. He doesn't need us to tell him he was wrong." When our conversation ends and I have hung up the phone, I let out a good scream. It feels good, so I let out another one.

James' mother calls a few days later, also to thank me, and to tell me that James has begun therapy, and that they will participate in this therapy too. "It was really brave of you to come and see us," she says.

The next suicide gesture comes some weeks later. Patricia is talking to her friend Maggie on the phone. "I have just taken a half a bottle of pills," she tells Maggie, who lives across the bay.

"Just a minute, my mom is on the other line," Maggie says. She puts Patricia on hold and dials 911, giving them Patricia's address. She gets back on the line and continues the conversation. Soon Patricia hears the ambulance sirens, but the ambulance cannot find her house, so Maggie hangs up and calls James' mother, who lives quite close to Patricia. James' mother goes to her house immediately and takes her to the emergency room. Right before having her stomach pumped, Patricia admits that while she took half the bottle of pills, there were only two pills in the bottle, so she actually only took one pill. They keep her for observation and send her home. We follow up and get her into therapy. "I wanted to see what Maggie would do," she says. "I wanted to see if she was really my friend."

Meanwhile, we have the faculty meeting and the parent meeting on suicide prevention. I still seem to be forever on the phone. Soon Kerry will be released from the hospital. The school wants her to transfer to another school. We are five months away from graduation, but they want her to start all over at another school. Frank and I dig in our heels. No. She has been here for two and a half years. All her friends are here, and she needs her friends. She has a good rapport with her teachers. The rest of the students need to see her returning to school and to a normal life. If she disappears, there will be no closure here. The school agrees to consider keeping her, but we need to arrange for a big summit meeting that includes Kerry, her father, her therapist, her father's therapist, the supervising psychiatrist, a counselor representing the district, the school counselor, the principal, Nancy, Margo, Frank and me. It takes a long time, but after much discussion and reassurance that Kerry has adequate support, we win. After another period of intense counseling while she is living at home, she will be allowed to return to school and graduate with her class. We agree to have Margo and the peer counselors at school the week she returns, in order to help everyone adjust.

The next suicide gesture comes in writing. A student describes in her journal about two attempts she has made. This also surprises me, because she is such a good student, she seems so well-adjusted. But when we talk, I uncover some serious stress in the family, and some emotional abuse, so we work with her and her family until they too are safely in therapy.

Before Kerry returns to school, Margo speaks to each class about the importance of staying true to one's feelings. "If you didn't like her before, you don't have to like her now," she says. "If you are her friend, just continue with normal life. You can talk to her about anything you want."

"What if she does it again?" someone asks.

"We have a pretty good support system set up here," Margo explains. "But, ultimately, nobody can prevent someone else from committing suicide if they really want to. Remember everything you have learned so far—tell an adult if you see any of the signs, in Kerry or in anybody else. But if something happens, it is not your fault."

On the day Kerry comes back to school we arrange for her to begin the day in Frank's art class. By now most of the students have seen and visited with Kerry outside the school setting, so they are not seeing her for the first time. Margo is there, I am there, and a peer counselor from McAteer High School is there in case anybody needs to talk about how they are feeling. We have sort of an overkill support system set up. I am nervous. Kerry is nervous. But she comes in as though nothing has happened, and the students all seem comfortable and natural, so I just sit and visit with the other counselors. When she goes to get her art portfolio, she joins a group and starts chatting with others. I feel like a person whose unreliable car has just started up.

The next weeks and months continue in a relatively normal manner. We keep close tabs on our five suicide gestures, we keep watch for others, we continue our support for other students, but things seem smoothed out.

In June, Frank and I sit in the balcony of the auditorium and watch the eighth graders march across the stage to get their diplomas. It is our tradition to sneak the seventh graders into the balcony to watch their friends graduate, even though the bulletin says not to bring students. Every year the principal sees us up there, but he never says anything. I am always teary at graduation, but this year I am more so. As the last student walks across the stage and the school band gets ready to play, I turn to Frank and say, "Well, they're all alive."

The Glass Doll And The Music Box
BY KERRY

It was a small blue-grey music box. The inside was lined with black felt. In the center was a glass doll; a dancer. It was clear glass with a painted face, hair, tu-tu & point shoes. She stood in fifth position, arms extended, bowing slightly. She stood on a spring and turned when the box was wound. The music it made was a faint, fabricated, eerie, rhythmical, ringing. This is its story.

In the year 1904 a girl lived with her mother and father. She was very shy and mostly kept to herself. It was probably because of her parents. They were very strict. She didn't like her parents but was very afraid of them. A friend of her mother's had recently died and they went to the cemetery. Her parents told her to wait by the entrance. A while after her parents had left she noticed something poking out of the ground. It was a small blue-grey music box. She scratched away the dirt and pulled it up. When her parents came she hid it behind her back. Her parents talked to each other the whole way home so they did not notice or ask about the music box. The girl went immediately up to her room and placed it on her end table. When she went to bed she opened it, wound it and went to bed. The box began to play its slow eerie tune as the dancer turned slowly and the girl dropped off to sleep. It took up to a month or more before it started to happen. But slowly, slowly, it began to take effect. The girl would lie in bed, the music would play and it seemed to her that the music came from somewhere deep inside her head and not from the music box at all. It seemed like it was going out rather than coming in.

The song began to pound in her head. She felt nervous, angry, frightened, and a mix of emotions. Run, scream, cry, laugh, anything, and then she would fall asleep. It became worse. Her head hurt worse now and it hurt all the time. She never said anything and she kept winding the box every night, even when she didn't want to. It was like a drug; she couldn't stop. Then one night while she lay in bed and the box played, the pounding and the aching seemed to come from her whole body. In the pain her ear drums burst and blood dripped from her ears.

She sat up and in her horror saw that the expression on the doll had changed to an evil grin. As if a puppet controlled by strings, she got up from the bed and broke a piece of her mirror. She walked to her parents' room and walked in. She slit her mother's throat before she had a chance to scream, and pushed the piece of glass into her father's chest and left the room. She went back to her room and laid down. She was found the next morning, said to have died of a heart attack. The house was cleaned and the music box was placed in the attic.

Eighty years later the family that lived in the same house was cleaning out the attic. They also had a daughter. In the corner she found a blue-grey music box. She took it to her room. At bedtime she put the box on her dresser top, wound it and opened it. The box began to play its slow, eerie tune as the dancer turned slowly and the girl dropped off to sleep . . .

11. Screaming in My Car

Hallie, now a sophomore in high school, calls me. She has been invited to a costume party celebrating the first day of spring and she wants to talk about symbols of the season. At the end of our conversation, I ask her how school is going. "Not so well, Judy," she says. "I just got a 2.6 on my report card."

I am really surprised, because Hallie is among the most obviously smart and creative students I have ever had, and I tell her so. "What is going on?" I ask. "You're a straight-A student."

"I've just stopped trying," she says. "It's really boring. In English we've been studying Fitzgerald forever. I guess I'm just tired of studying about the emotional problems of middle-aged white men. And my history class is worse. I mean, my history teacher actually skipped over all the chapters in our book that weren't about Europe."

Madeline, one of my outstanding sixth graders, is leaving school a few weeks early. Her parents help run a Buddhist retreat to which the family needs to move in May. They give me lots of advance notice, so I have some lessons for her to take with her, and she'll receive full credit for the year. But I will miss her. This is my last month of school, too, since I am planning on a one-year sabbatical. On Madeline's last day, I ask her to stay after class a moment, and I give her a good-bye card and a glass marble for her to look at and remember us by. "I'll really miss you," I say. She looks troubled, and gets a bit defensive. "I can't help it, I have to leave, my family needs to move."

"Yes, I know," I reassure her. "You have good reason to leave. It is okay for you to go. And it's okay for me to miss you."

"Anyway," she says, with just a trace of resentment, " you're going too. You'll be gone for a whole year."

"Yes," I say. "And it is okay for me to go, too. And it's okay for you to miss me. " We smile at each other.

Suzanne is our audio-visual clerk. She does all the duplicating of material for teachers, types out all the bulletins, and orders movies, videos and tapes for us. Her office is in a far corner of the third floor and it is the place where all teachers go when they need supplies, copies of last-minute lesson plans, hugs, candy, Kleenex to dry tears, and a sympathetic heart. It is the kind of human hearth that could never exist next door to the principal's office. In fact, feminist scholars could write a great article analyzing Suzanne's office and the principal's office as marginal and central politics.

One year Suzanne, who had never been to Europe, planned to go to Paris in the summer. But when we had lunch with her one day in December, she told us she just didn't have the money to travel and also pay her rent, since she was unemployed every summer. One teacher who was also going to be in Paris wanted to meet her at a famous restaurant for lunch. "If you purchase your ticket before December 10th," he told her, "it will only cost you $560." But Suzanne said she just couldn't afford it.

When we returned to school, my friend Kathie said to me, "You know, Judy, if we could just get ten people to donate fifty dollars, we could buy that ticket for Suzanne for Christmas."

"What a great idea," I said. "We'll certainly donate, we only have to find eight more people." Kathie had a class, but I had time to run around the school and share this idea. I got more than eight people, easily. The principal contributed immediately. Some people gave more than fifty dollars. The next day, I took checks to the bank and got nine one-hundred dollar bills. Kathie and I made a big mural, with a crowd of people waving goodbye on a piece of land labeled "San Francisco." In the air, a red-headed Suzanne looked out of an airplane window. In Paris, our friend Deborah, who used to teach with us, was standing by the Eiffel Tower waving hello. We stapled an envelope labeled "Cab Fare" to the San Francisco part. It contained $100. We stapled an envelope labeled "Airfare" to the plane. It held $600. We stapled an envelope labeled "Lunch Money" near Paris. It held $200. We invited everyone who had contributed to come to our room at the beginning of lunch. I stopped by Suzanne's room and casually asked her to come by. She seemed surprised to see all these people in my room. I turned her around to look at the mural. "Merry Christmas, Suzanne," we said, and I shoved a chair under her just in time as she collapsed in shock. We all cried. It was one of those great *It's A Wonderful Life* moments.

This year, while I was on sabbatical, Suzanne's job was changed. She could work for the teachers only two periods a day. The rest of her day she had to work as a secretary for a federal program in our school. Then the new principal decided she didn't want Suzanne so far away from the central office, so she decided to move her downstairs. Teachers protested, but the principal didn't change her mind. Suzanne decided to quit her job after twenty years at our school and to move back to Texas, rather than to move downstairs by the central offices.

We teachers lost the only person in the school whose full

time job it was to give us direct help. And, because of the person she was, Suzanne gave us love and emotional support as well. No more last minute help, no more hugs, no more safe place to go cry. Most of the teachers, myself included, were devastated by this loss.

After Suzanne left, the already overloaded vice-principal spent an hour each morning duplicating teacher material. This one hour was supposed to replace what it took Suzanne a whole day to do. If teachers didn't get their materials in before eight o'clock, the work didn't get done. The downtown office, gearing up for massive cuts in employment, refused to refill Suzanne's position.

My friend Kathie told me that one day, while she was picking up some material she had had run off, two students from the Filipino bilingual program brought some work that Mr. P. wanted duplicated. The VP started yelling at them. "*I told you yesterday this was too much work to do.*" Before the students could leave, he grabbed the packet Mr. P had sent up to be copied and dumped it in the wastebasket.

I worry about how it will be, returning to school without Suzanne there.

Natis, the boy who made the wonderful enameled moon mobile in my "Moon, Moon" class, has been expelled from Reed College. He sat in at the President's office, protesting investments in South Africa, and refused to leave.

Nan, the girl who made the Moon Goddess costume, dropped out of high school. But she continues her artwork and she has her own radio program on a local station.

Belinda, one of my outstanding writers also dropped out of high school. I hear this story years later when I meet her on the street. She wrote an essay for her English class. The teacher gave it an F because it was too good. "I have never met a fourteen-year-old girl who could think," he writes, "and I don't think I've met one now. You must have copied this." She asks him to call her former teachers, but he refuses. Her mother comes to school and speaks to the counselor. Finally, she is given a "C". The next year, when her history teacher says that while he does not condone assassination, it was in a way a fortunate thing that Harvey Milk, a gay supervisor, was killed with Mayor Moscone, because gay politics were becoming too powerful in San Francisco. Belinda decides high school is not for her. She works for a while, takes the equivalency exam when she is old enough, and enters college.

As part of the business/education partnership program, Pacific Telephone Company, or "Pac Bell," has adopted our school. One of their officers comes to a faculty meeting and is very upbeat about the possibilities of this partnership. "Think about what you need," he tells us. "The sky is the limit."

Now, at this time, I am involved in a three-year research project with the Center for Research on Writing at UC Berkeley. All of my sixth graders' writing is sent to this center, copied, and then mailed to the University of London and to Kate Chapman, a teacher in northern London who will be my research partner. All of her class's writing is sent to us, having also been copied by the same universities. The idea is to give an expanded audience for the students' work. It takes weeks for the mail to go back and forth. There are five teachers from the Bay Area and five teachers in London involved in this project. All the other teachers, including Kate, have computers, modems, and software that enable them to communicate directly and immediately without using the mail service. I have computers in my classroom. The center offers me software and a modem.

All I need is a phone, and then Kate and I and our students can avoid all the mail expense and delay.

Since the sky is the limit, and since our school has just been adopted by a telephone company, it makes sense to me to ask Pac Bell for a telephone. I write a letter in September to the man in charge of the partnership program. I explain how my students can send a letter, a story, or a report, and it will be read by their writing partners in London the very next day if only I have a telephone.

I never hear from him. My principal hears from him, however, and comes to explain to me that there are overseas communication laws, and that PacBell cannot possibly grant me an overseas connection. No problem, I tell him enthusiastically. UC Berkeley already has the overseas connection. I just need to connect with Berkeley, and they will send my work on to Kate.

I don't hear anything for a long time. When I approach the principal again, he tells me that everyone is worried about being unfair. " We don't want to give one teacher something that will make another teacher feel bad," he says.

"But I am the only teacher in the school involved in this project," I say. "I go to Berkeley once a month for meetings. I have student researchers and observers in my classroom frequently. It involves a lot of extra work. I don't get paid for this—couldn't I at least get a phone? If other teachers complain, you could explain that it is because I am part of this research project."

"What we're going to do," he tells me, "is set up a committee. This committee will begin meeting after Christmas vacation, and we are going to design a form for teachers to fill out so they can request things from Pac Bell."

"But I already have my request," I say. "I already know what I want." "Fine," he says. "When the form comes out, you can fill it in."

"But that will be February," I say. "School is over in June. How long will it take after the form is filled out?"

At Christmas time, Pac Bell gives every child in our school candy canes, pens, and pads of paper. Each teacher gets a bottle of wine.

Some teachers take their classes to Pac Bell and get tours of the plant and great lunches. Bigwigs from PacBell come to tour our school, and I love it when they come to my class. "Oh, class," I say, "here are the people from the telephone company who are going to help us get our phone!" We explain our research project and the history of our request. Pretty soon they take my classroom off the guided tour.

I never get the phone. Sometimes I laugh about this. PacBell adopted our school and the sky was the limit and I couldn't get a phone. Sometimes I drive around in my car and scream.

After their first five days at Lick Wilmerding, a private high school in San Francisco, Beverly, Gail and Ellen return to visit and tell me and my colleague Frank sternly, "You taught us wrong." Frank and I sit down with them to listen to their complaints. "Our teachers begin class by going around the room and asking questions like, what is the capitol city of some place, or what date did something or other happen. The kids from private schools know all these answers and we don't."

"Hm," I say, "I am sorry that is happening to you. I can imagine how it must feel, but you know a lot more than you think that you know right now. Your time here has not been spent memorizing facts. You are all very sophisticated thinkers, your creative selves are alive and well, you are each skilled writers. You express yourselves brilliantly. My hunch is that in six weeks you will be the top students in the class. It will be much easier for you to catch up and memorize facts than it will be for the other students to learn how to think and express themselves well. When it is time to write essays, analyze literature, or discuss ideas, you three will excel, I'm sure. Please come back in six weeks and let me know what happens."

But it doesn't take six weeks. At our open house in the beginning of October, Beverly says sheepishly, "You were right. Now we're getting A's. I'm sorry we said those things to you."

Last fall I visited Beverly at Harvard where she is a freshman. Together we attended a panel discussion led by Peggy McIntosh on The Female Student at Harvard. I was shocked to hear story after story of sexual harassment. I worry that Jessica's middle school years might have been her last opportunity to study in a setting where the experiences of women and people of color were often central in the curriculum.

When it is time to ask questions during a student-of-the-week interview, Jody makes an unkind remark about the student being interviewed. She teases him about being gay. It is the third or fourth time that I have had to speak to her about making comments in class about people's sexual identity. I tell her to go to the counseling office. After class, I go there to find that she never went—she just went on to her next class. When I explain the problem to her counselor, he decides to send her home to return with a parent. This is a Friday. On Monday morning, someone comes into a meeting at eight o'clock to tell me that Jody's mother is waiting in my room. She is treasurer of the PTA, I have met her many times, and I consider her a friend. But when I get to my room, I see that she is furious with me. "I can't believe that I have had to get up out of a sick bed and come to school because you have a problem with my child calling other people faggots," she said. "I have adolescents hanging around my house all the time, and they are always calling each other gay and teasing each other. If you don't know this about adolescents, you have no business teaching this age." She stops yelling and starts crying. I get the Kleenex. Jody is having a good time watching this interaction between her mother and her teacher.

"First of all," I say, "I didn't send Jody home, her counselor did. I sent her to the office and she never went there, so that is why her counselor requested your presence today. Second, I don't have a say in what your daughter or her friends do in your home, but in this class it is not okay to tease people about being homosexual, or to use it as a put-down."

The parent is furious. Sometimes she is yelling at me, sometimes she is crying. She looks as though she could hit me. My friend Kathie is at the other end of the room pacing back and forth, trying to figure out how to help me. This parent is hysterical and her daughter is having a great time watching the drama. The parent says, "I see all this material about women, I know you teach about women, I think you have a very serious personal problem. I think you are taking what my daughter said very personally, and I think you are punishing her for your own problems. You have no business teaching."

"So," I say, "are you saying that you think I am a lesbian?"

"I didn't say that," she sniffs.

"Look," I say. "San Francisco has a written policy. We do not allow racial slurs, ethnic slurs, or homophobic slurs in the classroom. It's as simple as that. I consider sexual slurs to be as serious as racial slurs. But I know you're feeling sick today (several times she has mentioned having the flu), so why don't you go home and reschedule an appointment with the counselor at another time when you are feeling better." She finally leaves, looking up to the last minute like she might slug me.

First I go to the bathroom and cry. Kathie comes to comfort me. "What a horrible experience," she says. "You didn't need this to start your day." Then I go to find the principal so he will get Jody and speak to her before she gleefully reports her mother's accusations to the whole class. He does. Eventually she tells everyone anyway, but at least I get a little time.

A week or so later, Jody's mother makes an appointment with the counselor. It's my birthday. I tell the counselor that it's my birthday. "For a present," I ask, "don't make me sit through a meeting with Jody's mother." "Don't worry, I'll handle it, happy birthday," he tells me. Later, he says that she began the meeting by saying, "I owe Ms. Logan an apology." Well, she got that right, I tell him, and I thank him. He read her the city rule about slurs. By this time, her daughter is also in trouble for carving her initials in a school violin. She finally gets it that just because many adolescents participate in sexual put-downs, it is not okay. Our job as parents and teachers is to correct that behavior.

Several weeks later I deliver something to the main office, and Jody's mother is there. "Can I speak to you for a moment?" she asks. Oh no, not without a counselor to mediate, I think. But I say, "This is my prep period and I have a lot of errands to run, but if you make an appointment with the counselor I'll be happy to meet with you."

"This will only take a moment," she says, sitting down on the bench outside of the principal's office. I sit down too, gingerly. Ready to bolt.

"I want to apologize for my behavior in your classroom," she says. I think to myself, don't say it is okay, because it was not okay. I just sit and listen. She continues, "I mean, what you are trying to do is really heroic. I'm sorry I gave you such a bad time."

"Yes," I smile, "what I am trying to do *is* really heroic. Thank you for your apology."

A parent of one of my students is really good at making me feel that no matter what I do, I am not doing enough. Although her son isn't completing his work and seems disrespectful, somehow our parent conferences always seem to drift towards what I should be doing differently, rather than to what her son, Jake, should be doing differently. So today, as I walk downstairs to the counseling office to meet with her, armed with my grade book, I am determined that I will be calm and professional and not let her rattle me. I enter the office and smile. Intending to talk about Jake's grades, I fumble and say, "I am here to discuss Grake's jades."

Peggy looks sad and asks to speak to me as she is leaving class. "Sure," I tell her, "go sit on the couch and I'll be right there." After hall duty, I join her. "What's up?" I ask.

"I have a problem in my science class," she says. " My teacher gave a test. We were supposed to supply definitions. For the definition of 'Homo sapiens,' I put 'humankind.' He marked it wrong and didn't give me any points, and said I should have put 'mankind.'" I comfort her and ask Frank to talk to the science teacher, as I figure he will listen to Frank better than to me. Frank does, but the teacher doesn't change his policy.

The next year when this same thing happens to Shoshannah, however, she writes a great research report on the uses of *humankind* versus *mankind*, legitimizing the word and changing his mind at last.

Another teacher, who is now retired, used to begin his math classes by announcing that research showed that girls didn't do very well in math, so they shouldn't worry about it too much. After all, boys didn't do very well in English. When the students tell me this, I say, "Oh, right, Faulkner and Shakespeare were pretty terrible writers, I guess there's no chance for girls to do well in math or science either." I talk to the teacher about what he is saying. He is polite but does not change. He makes this same announcement year after year.

One day Lia looks depressed. She is a straight-A student. "What's wrong?" I ask.

"I just got something wrong on my science test," she says.

"What?" I ask.

"Well, the test was on class rules. It was a fill-in test. The question was, 'The legs of your chair should be on the yellow blank,' and I wrote *line*."

"What was the correct answer?" I ask.

"It should have been, 'The legs of your chair should be on the yellow *mark*.'" (This teacher has painted yellow lines — sorry, marks — on his floor so the students' desks will be lined up in neat rows.)

"Oh, Lia," I say sadly.

Arthur, a sixth grader, has a very hard time sitting still. Every day I read to the class after lunch, and every day Arthur has to be reminded to stop drumming his pencil on the table, or to stop swinging a yoyo around, or to refrain from getting up in the middle of the story to look out the window. I am sympathetic to his need to move around, but consistent in my request that he sit and listen for fifteen minutes each day. On this day, Arthur is tapping his pencil on the table. I stop reading. "Arthur, please put your pencil away," I say. He pretends to do so. A few minutes later he is tapping away again. This time I just stop reading and wait for him to put away the pencil. He reaches under his desk for his backpack. But once under the desk, Arthur seems distracted and totally absorbed in his backpack, forgetting the rest of the class. He begins to play with something. Now, Arthur's desk is right in front of my teacher stool, where I perch to read stories. He may think he is invisible, but I can see everything he is doing. One hand seems to be stuck in his backpack. He twists around to try to reach the other hand into his back pocket, but he can't quite make it. He goes through amazing contortions. I watch his struggles, trying to figure it out. Finally, I say calmly, "Arthur, did you accidentally handcuff yourself?"

"Yes," he says.

"Well come up here and I'll help you get loose." He turns around so I can get the keys out of his back pocket, and I unlock the handcuffs. He returns sheepishly to his seat, and I resume my reading, but after a few minutes I burst out laughing. "Arthur, I'm not laughing at you,' I say, "but that was such a great example of how hard it is for you to sit still." Arthur laughs with me. The class laughs. How many people accidentally handcuff themselves when they are supposed to be sitting quietly? A few weeks later we are walking through the Oakland Museum on our way to a special exhibit. Arthur is by my side as we walk through a section of medieval-looking restraints, including iron chains and leg irons. "I'm glad you didn't have those in your backpack," I say, and we laugh again.

My eighth grade students come in from lunch very distressed. There is a rumor going around the yard that the faculty has determined a dress code for graduation. The students are angry. I haven't heard anything about it, but it is clear that it would be foolish to put anything but this on the agenda for today's lesson. We telephone the main office and ask an administrator or counselor to come to our room to explain what is going on. "Yes," the counselor tells us, "there is a dress code that is going to be strictly enforced. No off-the-shoulder dresses, no black dresses, no strapless dresses, no gloves, no hats, no heels higher than two inches, no tuxedos—" I can't remember all the "nos."

Students are very unhappy. After they have time to talk about their feelings, they talk about what they can do. Maggie, in particular, is upset. "I already bought my dress, and it's off the shoulder," she cries. "I spent my own money on it, and I'm not sure I can exchange it, since it came from a thrift shop."

"Maybe your parents can write a letter," I suggest, but Maggie decides to talk to her counselor. She is crying.

The counselor takes her to the principal. The principal tells her to bring the dress to school the next day, to put it on, and to come to his office. He will look at it and decide if it is appropriate for graduation. The next day, Maggie brings her pink lace dress to school. She puts it on in the bathroom. She comes to my room first for moral support. I am having a very hard time, sending her off to parade in front of the principal. "Tell me everything he says," I say.

Maggie and her counselor go to the principal's office. She stands in front of his desk. "You look very pretty," he tells her. "The dress will be fine, you may wear it. Now, Maggie, don't tell anyone else that I made a special case for you. Don't tell anyone else about our talk."

"Oh," she says, "I've already promised Ms. Logan that I will tell her everything you say."

"That's all right," he says, "you may tell Ms. Logan, but don't tell other students."

When she returns to my room, she says that the principal said that if someone wears a tuxedo, he will still let him graduate off stage, but he is hoping that this rule will prevent people from doing so.

How unfair, I think. It is the person who follows the rule, then, who will be punished. I think about what we are teaching our children. Make secret deals with the principal. Ignore rules instead of working together to change them. I wonder why all this energy is being expended on what students wear to graduation. I think it is a class issue. The majority of our students are students of color. Many of them are on welfare. For some of them, graduation from eighth grade is a major family celebration. They wear tuxedos and formal dresses; they are clearly sexually mature. Others still wear slacks and shirts, or cotton dresses and flats. But the administration is very uncomfortable with this diversity. "You are not graduating as an individual," the principal says frequently, "you are graduating as a class." It is interesting to me that we are a school that prides ourselves on our diversity, but we want everyone to look alike. The next year, the principal asks for and receives PTA funding to buy the eighth grade class graduation gowns. No more arguments about what to wear.

We are in the school library, beginning our research for the quilt honoring women in American history. The librarian is looking on as I give some preliminary instructions, The principal walks in and is also looking on. Ruby raises her hand. "Ms. Logan, don't you think you are excluding the boys by giving yet another lesson centering on women?"

"No, Ruby, I don't," I say, and I finish my instructions. But two of Ruby's girlfriends have nodded their heads in agreement at her question, so later I take the three of them aside to talk to them. "Let's see," I say, "we did the NOW essay contest, and now we're doing the quilt. That is two lessons that center on women. This is your history we are talking about, but I take it you think I'm being excessive?"

"What about Black History Month?" she says.

"We did men and women on that assignment," I reply. But the girls still seem resistant, angry. Ruby says, "I don't know, Ms.

Logan, I feel that I am learning too much about women, and not enough about men, especially men of color." Her friend, Jocylyn, chimes in, "And I feel that I don't know enough about George Washington."

"Well," I reply, "Mr. Foreman and I plan your curriculum in three year segments. Some things are stressed in sixth grade, global and national things are stressed in seventh and eighth grade. You have seen my India bulletin board in class. Next year when you are in seventh grade, you will be studying women and men in other countries, like India."

"Yes," they say, "but you won't be here." Hmmm. Obviously I'm not going to be able to just slip out on this sabbatical without being taken to task for it. "That's true," I say. "I won't be here. But someone else will be here to teach the seventh grade curriculum. And I will be back when you are eighth graders." I wonder to myself whether they will punish me in their eighth-grade year too.

The next day, I hand Ruby a stack of pictures of men of color. "Here, Ruby, you are in charge of putting these around the room." When I go to pick up a movie I have ordered for the day, I see that there is a ten-minute film on George Washington. I bring it to class, and before I show it I say, "This movie is dedicated to Justine." The class watches it dutifully, Jocelyn and I flash each other a look. Mine says, See? I listen to what you say, be careful what you wish for. Hers says, Lighten up, I get it.

12. How to Keep Heart

Today my next-door neighbor and principal of a middle school considered to be one of the "toughest" middle schools in San Francisco (translate "poor and African American"), told me about a full-time resource position available at her school. I was tempted to apply, because I am tired.

But I don't believe in resource teachers. Or, I should say, I don't believe in the *position* of resource teachers, since I know a lot of terrific resource teachers personally. Resource teachers have no classes assigned to them. A resource teacher spends five periods a day helping classroom teachers by teaching model lessons in their classes, finding books and materials they might need, helping them to come up with strategies for individual students or particular lessons, and feeding them ideas.

But I believe that the heart of the educational process is in the daily classroom connection that is woven between teacher and students. Education is not something that you can separate from this day-to-day process. It builds on itself and the hundreds of insights that a teacher gains from this daily process is the warp through which the threads of education must be woven. No matter how dynamic a particular lesson is, it remains only a particular lesson if it tries to exist outside the context of the daily classroom continuum.

I have seen great teachers leave the classroom to become resource teachers. To me, this is like taking a great parent, a mother, for example, and separating her from her children so that she can travel from family to family in order to model good parenting, or to cook for them, or to read the bedtime story, or to choose the elementary school for the younger children. *There is no way that this can work.* Yes, she can be a help from time to time, yes, she might even make some children think, "I wish my mother were like her," but by cutting herself off from her own family, she has done more damage than she can possibly repair by being of help to others.

By separating oneself from the daily experience of being a classroom teacher, a resource teacher loses touch with the powerful unexpectedness of the day-to-day opportunities to validate growth that have nothing to do with materials, techniques, or frameworks. The ongoing *process* of the classroom is the heart of the school, and I have never seen a resource teacher, no matter how talented, brilliant, or dedicated she or he may be, who has not eventually "lost heart."

Knowing this makes me somewhat sad, because I am tired. I do not want to "lose heart" by leaving the classroom, but I don't want to die of a heart attack, either.

At the root of the problem here is that the classroom teacher is frequently seen as being on the bottom of a hierarchical pyramid. To be offered a job as a resource teacher is to be offered a "step up." To get out of the classroom is seen as gaining prestige and power. But I don't see it that way. I think that to disconnect myself from daily contact with a particular group of students is to marginalize myself in an unacceptable way, and to cut myself off from the joy of the educational process that can occur only in a long, given stretch of time.

My suggestion, in order to "keep heart" and to avoid heart attacks, is to eliminate the position of resource teacher, and to take those periods of time (five or six a day) and distribute them to the individual classroom teachers. Each classroom teacher would become her or his own resource person, and the resource person would become a classroom teacher. Instead of teaching five classes a day with thirty-two to thirty-six students in each class, the teacher would teach four classes, and have one period to collect his/her own materials, ideas, and strategies. This would diminish the idea of an "expert" helping those who are then seen as "not expert," which is in itself somewhat divisive and hierarchical.

Also, this plan would address the overworked, exhausted state of the classroom teacher. One does not have to do something twenty-four hours a day in order to prove that one can do it well. This hierarchical, unspoken assumption that the classroom teacher is somehow on the bottom rung of the educational ladder leads to the assumption that pull-out programs and resourcing will somehow help make things better. We are trying to patch that which we ourselves have damaged by not acknowledging the importance of the daily classroom experience.

In the state of California, because of the disastrous state of our educational budget, I worry about a trend towards making even more programs—such as GATE and Special Ed—pullout programs, further disrupting the continuity of the classroom.

Continuity and long range planning are vital to this experience. If an "expert" teacher comes into the classroom to do a dynamite lesson on, say, descriptive writing and this lesson is really terrific (and it usually is), it makes the students sad that this doesn't happen every day, and it leaves the teacher demoralized because she or he doesn't have the time and resources to create that kind of dynamite production on a daily basis.

Or the resource teacher comes in with a whole different set of student expectations from the classroom teacher. (Raise your hand before you speak/Don't raise your hand before you speak. Don't interrupt each other/Speak your mind out loud and clear. Sit on the floor and make yourself comfortable in the classroom/Sit up straight at your desk at all times. Compete, compete/Cooperate, cooperate.) The classroom teacher then either has to back up a whole set of rules and expectations that she doesn't agree with, or she has to be willing to pit herself against the resource teacher, who is supposed to be there to help her. One of the arguments for having a resource teacher is that he or she is given an amount of time—say, one day a week and/or parts of each day—to familiarize herself with lots of materials, ideas, strategies, techniques, etc. She then has a real smorgasbord to offer the teacher that the teacher does not have time to prepare herself, given her lack of time and energy for such things. But I see this as a serious drawback. First of all, the resource teacher begins to think of materials in isolation from students and the process of learning. Any classroom teacher knows that an idea that worked at ten o'clock on Friday doesn't necessarily work at eleven o'clock on Friday, or that materials that worked really well last year just might bomb out this year. The process of education is dynamic and has a mysterious element; it cannot be reduced to charts of skills or lists of books or even to frameworks of ideas. It is all of those things and much more. So the resource teacher is diminished by being divided from this mystery, and can be tempted to overemphasize the things of education, losing touch with the process.

And the classroom teacher is diminished by not being honored with the time to work out her own creative solutions to the problems of her classroom. To remedy this problem, I see ten teachers being given one resource period a day, as well as time each week to share ideas and materials with others teaching in her field, instead of two full time resource teachers in a school.

This keeps good teachers in direct relationships with students, and also provides opportunities for them to share with others.

Twelve or fifteen years ago I proposed this idea at my own school. I was put on a committee to study all the possibilities for a year. We did so, and gave a thorough report on the advantages of classroom teachers being their own resource teachers. But this plan is more difficult for administrators to manage. We were told that the plan was not feasible because of paychecks. The resource teacher was paid from federal funds, the classroom teachers were paid from city funds. It was too complicated to try to get five twenty percent paychecks from the government instead of one full time one. So much for a year on a committee.

Another argument for having a resource teacher is that not all teachers are good, so at least this way, students will get one good lesson from the resource teacher every week or two. But I see it differently. If that great resource teacher were in the classroom, students would be getting a dynamic education every day, not just every week. Although education pretends to be the great equalizer, we have always had some teachers who are better than other ones, but the solution to this is not to siphon off the good ones, to "reward them" by taking them out of the classroom, but rather to nurture and inspire the not-so-good ones. In my twenty-five years of observing teaching, I have noticed the tendency of administrators to bring pressure to bear on outstanding teachers, not on mediocre ones.

Another problem in this hierarchical view of things is that resource teachers can be seen by classroom teachers as "other." They are perceived as tools of the administration. Administrators reluctant to deal directly with teacher ideas or teacher problems can be tempted to use the resource people as buffers. Resource teachers can easily get caught in between.

However, if every teacher in the school were four-fifths class-room teacher and one-fifth resource teacher, these divisions would disappear, and better communication would take place all around.

13. Beyond the Curriculum Guide

I t is thirty years ago, 1966. I am a new teacher teaching in a junior high in the Hunter's Point/Bayview district of San Francisco. Ninety-four percent of the student body is African American, and more than half of the students live in public housing. The curriculum guide, the document from the central office that dictates what books will be taught in each grade, tells me that I am to teach Lamb's *Tales from Shakespeare* to my eighth grade classes.

Ooohhh, they're going to hate this, I think. So I find a quote by Bertrand Russell that says that school ruins Shakespeare for kids. If they could only meet him in the flesh, he says, full of jollity and ale. I climb on my teacher stool and share the quote. "How does school ruin things you love?" I ask. I get a lot of examples. We have a great discussion. "Well, school sometimes does that to Shakespeare too," I say, "which is really a shame because he wrote a lot of interesting stuff." I tell them a little about Shakespeare's life, about his passion for plays. "Shakespeare found stories in lots of places and turned them into plays," I explain. "Lamb took Shakespeare's plays and turned them back into stories. We are going to take these stories and turn them back into plays, just as Shakespeare did. Find a partner or a group to work with. You don't have to read all of Shakespeare's stories, but choose one that you want to turn into a play. At the end of this assignment we will have a Shakespeare Festival and you will each present your play."

I am amazed at how well this catches on. "Can we make posters to advertise our play?" Yes. "Can we put them up around the room?" Yes. "Can we bring stuff in for costumes and props?" Yes. "We are shy. We don't want to do a play in front of the class. Can we put ours on the tape recorder and just do a radio play?" Yes. "Can we do ours with puppets?" Yes. "We're having trouble figuring out how Shakespeare would have handled this scene . . . Can we look at his script to see how he did it?" Well, yes (!) "Our play takes place in Verona (or Troy, or Dunsinane, or Denmark). Can we make a map to show where that is?" Yes. Students from my remedial reading classes notice these posters and maps appearing in the room. "Can we do that too?" Sure.

The librarian from the Third Street Library calls me. "What have you done? All the books on Shakespeare are checked out of the library for the first time ever."

When it is time for our festival I am delighted with what the students have done. They come up with a marvelous mix of Shakespeare juxtaposed with Hunter's Point (read "Harlem," if you are unfamiliar with San Francisco). In *Julius Caesar*, for example, a student dressed in a white sheet, waving a cardboard sword, bellows "Friends, Romans, Countrymen, lend me your ears and I'll lower your taxes!"

Two students from Romeo and Juliet circle nose to nose and shoulder to shoulder. "You phony old Capulet," one says. "You jive ass Montague," the other one replies, "Your mother." It is not Laurence Olivier but they have the general idea. Students do a whole range of plays. After this festival we talk about what they have seen. ("What have you learned about Shakespeare?" "He wrote a lot about many different things about different times and different places. He's fun.") We learn about tragedies and comedies and history plays. When some agency offers our school free tickets to go see *Henry IV* Part One, all my students sign up.

At least I haven't done any damage, I think. We've survived the curriculum guide.

I am a new teacher and I have entered a school where the culture is almost totally unfamiliar to me. I am the only white person in the room. The curriculum says I am supposed to teach dictionary skills. "Pretend you are a person coming to the projects from New York," I say to the class. "You will be taking the bus to school, walking the halls, going to class, spending time on the playground. What are the words and phrases you might hear that would be unfamiliar to you but that you would need to understand in order to survive?" Students begin to list words and phrases like "Shining you on." That's like, you know, you're sitting on the bus looking out the window and you see your friend walking on the street but you pretend you don't." "Or you're eating something good and your friend asks for some and you just act like you didn't hear him. That's shining him on." Or: "That's tight. That means, like, stingy, or selfish, or cruel."

They sometimes give me more than one definition or example. We alphabetize this dictionary and number the definitions. We use this class dictionary as a prelude to our "real" dictionary lesson, and I, who am not from New York at all but from San Francisco, begin to learn about the culture of my students.

I am standing in front of this same class and we are supposed to be reading *Tom Sawyer,* and I am explaining how Samuel Clemens changed his name to Mark Twain but I am feeling terribly irrelevant to these children's lives. So I bring in some music that was popular during the sixties: "Oh Happy Day." Close your eyes and listen to this music and tell me what makes you happy, I say. We create a class poem on the board about happiness. I feel better.

Another memory of my first classroom: I take pictures of each class and have them blown up into posters and put them up around the room. The classroom finally reflects us. I put their classwork up on the bulletin boards next to their class poster.

It is the sixties and cities are rioting. One of our school's former students is shot and killed in Hunter's Point, and his body is left in a field for some hours before it is taken away. Our students see it on their way home from school. This high school student was a passenger in a stolen car, and was shot and killed as he fled the scene after police stopped the car. This was the incident that triggered the San Francisco riots.

In school the students write about what is happening. I discover that they all think the National Guard was called out to protect them from the police. I learn a lot. Students begin to write plays about the Black Panthers, with characters like Bobby Seale, Huey Newton, Angela Davis and Eldridge Cleaver. They fight over who gets to play each part.

Students come to school with axes, pokers, and knives. "I am glad you came to class," I say, "but leave all the weapons in the corner by the door."

I am teaching in this school when Martin Luther King is assassinated. We spend the day talking, crying and writing a memorial booklet.

A few months later Bobby Kennedy is in California campaigning for the presidency. I have a mock election in my class, and I am shocked when Bobby Kennedy loses. "Why is this?" I ask, "I know you really like Bobby Kennedy—he visited the projects here just weeks ago, he is very popular. How did he lose this election?"

"If we vote him in they will just kill him," the students say. This happens in all of my classes. I am shocked and saddened. I give my talks about hope and faith; that just because it happened to Martin Luther King and John Kennedy doesn't mean it will happen to everyone you care about.

I come home and talk about this at the dinner table. "What can I do to turn this around?" I say to my husband, and I go to bed early, depressed and exhausted. Later, he comes in and shakes my shoulder.

"Honey, wake up, Bobby Kennedy has just been shot." "That's not funny," I say, and roll over. "Get up," he says, "I'm not kidding." I am up for hours, hoping Kennedy will live, and I return to school the next day and face my students. They are kind and do not say "I told you so."

I am a beginning teacher and this class gives me a running account every day of how I'm doing. "You doing good, teacher, but wait till Donald Lance gets here, then you're in trouble." "Those boots are nice, teacher, you doing just fine today, but wait till Donald Lance gets here." "The boys just like you cause you got a big butt, teacher, but I like you cause you're nice. I hope you do okay with Donald." "Teacher, did you make that dress yourself? You put that zipper in by hand? Nice. Are you pregnant?"

Each day I take attendance and each day Donald Lance is absent and each day the class warns me about him when I take roll. One day a very mature young man walks into class. He is probably only fifteen, but he seems to be about twenty-five.

(I am twenty-four.) He exudes rage. The class settles down to watch. I have never seen them so attentive. The student who must be Donald Lance walks to the back of the room and stands at the window.

"Class," I say, "please take your seats," although everyone is seated except the new student. "I cannot start class until everyone is seated." Pause. Donald continues to stare out the window. Finally, I say, "Donald, please sit down." And his rage explodes. He climbs on a chair and puts one foot on the table, he gives me the finger with both hands, and he starts yelling, "Fuck you, teacher, fuck you up your ass!!" The class watches me carefully. I have adrenalin coming out my ears. This child looks as though he would like to kill me, and could. I remember that at the new-teacher meeting on discipline, the dean said that we should send referrals down to the office with the student if at times something happened that we could not handle. This seems like one of those times. "Do not put generalities on the referral," the dean said, "Be specific."

So while Donald continues to yell and give me two fingers, I reach in my desk drawer for referrals and as calmly as possible I write, "When told to take his seat, Donald climbed on it and yelled, 'Fuck you teacher, fuck you up your ass.'" I fill out the homeroom, date, and time, and hold it out in my hand. I am trembling all over and the paper shakes. I am not a brave person. "Donald," I say, "please take this referral downstairs." And to my surprise, *he does*! I never see him again.

"You did good, teacher," the class tells me, but this incident never leaves me, and twenty-five years later I still worry about it.

I stayed at Bayview in Hunter's Point for five years. Everything I really needed to know about teaching I learned there. But each year I lost at least one student to a violent death—stabbings at parties, car accidents, shootings. The politics of the school and the community drained time and energy from good teaching. Finally I was offered a job at another middle school and I decided to transfer. My students gave me a farewell party, and said, "You going to a tough neighborhood, teacher, those Mission kids are *tough*, you better be careful."

Years later Kay asks me to take one of her special ed students into my classroom for one period a day. "He is really smart," Kay tells me, "and he would benefit a lot from your class discussions and projects." So I take Austin into class, and sure enough, he is really smart, but while he is great during discussions, he rarely does any work. Kay invites me to the next parent conference where I meet Austin's mother, who has several small children with her. She keeps looking at me. Finally she says, "Did you used to teach at Mission High School?" "No," I say, "but I taught at Bayview. "Yes," she says, "Ms. Logan," and we look at each other for a few moments as we begin to recognize each other. She is a former student; I am her former teacher. I feel some anxiety as I watch her assessing me. We are both remembering what Bayview was like. It was where I learned about institutional racism. The students referred to it as "The Jailhouse."

Austin's mother looks at me and says quietly, "You did the best you could."

One day I came home and announced to my friend Claudia that I had finished my book. "That's wonderful, Judy," she said. "Congratulations!" Then, after a pause, she asked, "How do you know you're finished?"

"Because it's the middle of June," I tell her. "All teachers know that if it's the middle of June we must be finished."

Afterword

U sually, it is "not done" to write the afterword to a book dedicated to oneself. But in the spirit of Judy Logan's own teaching, which so often raises the questions of "Why not?" and "What if . . . ?" I took up the unusual honor she offered. I see it as a chance to accept a gift and pass the gift along. Much of my own life history has this sequence, and perhaps much of our happier schooling in thought, emotion, and spirituality has this pattern of receiving and recognizing gifts, and passing those gifts along.

It takes my breath away to open a book on education and find it so peopled. In most educators' writing, I can't see a student for miles around. The mapped City of Educational Abstraction is not offering any hot lunches. I hear the sounds of cranes and trucks and pneumatic drills demolishing old structures for the further expansion of the city. But what happened to all the people?

Teaching Stories is richly peopled with students, parents, and teachers, living vividly in the moments of their lives. Over Judy Logan's shoulder you can see and hear them. She is the participating narrator. The classrooms and hallways never quiet down. The city beckons for another field trip. I can imagine why Logan's sixth, seventh, and eighth graders have wanted to read these chapters. These stories are theirs.

Most educational theorists refer to other educational theorists. In *Teaching Stories*, Judy Logan derives educational theory

155

from many years of immersion in intense, exciting classes. Her theories seem to me to be grounded and deftly presented in the language of the classroom. Using the students' own language, she writes of her balancing of the "have-to's" and the "get-to's"—by which she means the things students are required to do as against the ones in which they may follow their inclinations. She captures a whole paradigm shift in her dialogue with her five-year-old niece, who says, "Teachers know everything." "No. Teachers know some things. Nobody knows everything . . ." And later, as the Story of Two Quilts so tellingly illustrates, "Students have their own stories."

Most writing about education, together with most teaching, evades the matters which most frighten and confuse adults, which we are unable to "master." Judy Logan allows for discussion of these life matters as they arise in students' lives. Therefore, *Teaching Stories* has many frank, funny, poignant, and disturbing scenes. They result from one teacher's day-in-and-day-out commitment to what philosopher Jane Martin terms the three C's, needed beyond the three R's, in education: care, concern, and connection.

I wish that Judy Logan had been the teacher of our own children because she herself has such a gift for recognizing the intelligence, heart, and soul of a young person, and teaching to that with precision and split-second sensitivity. She teaches without condescension or evasion and with commitment to the growth and development of each student in her care.

Students have many economic, social, and emotional uncertainties which Judy Logan allows them to acknowledge and think through, as they negotiate their complex lives. The collaborating teachers of her school are shown in making effective networks of support for students. In times of crisis, these teachers may need to be comitted to keeping students alive. On a daily basis, the book shows teaching which respects the students' experiences of love, hate, cruelty, jealousy, hope, pleasure, intuition, and above all, creative imagination and intelligence.

Surviving the curriculum guide, as Logan puts it, is another kind of life challenge for teachers. Our students rarely want to come to school because of the content of the formal curriculum. They come to see their friends. They come because it is better than home or the street. But Judy Logan makes the curriculum interesting, varied, textured, so that it provides for each child, in the words of Emily Style, windows into the experience of others, and mirrors of the student's own reality and validity. The students feel co-ownership. The stories testify to prodigious learning.

Some educational theorists fear, or claim to fear, that pedagogical innovation and greater curricular inclusiveness will undermine U. S. educational standards. The "standards" now supposedly in effect have produced abysmally poor results, especially with regard to students' basic skills of reading, writing, use of numbers, critical thinking, and becoming decent citizens. I believe that Judy Logan's students do outstanding work in all of these areas, not despite her innovative teaching, but because of it.

For example, year after year, Judy Logan's students in anonymous judging sweep the prizes in the essay contest which hundreds of students from all over the city enter. And year after year they impress the students and teachers in the high schools and colleges they go on to attend. Year after year they have impressed me, as I have met them or heard from them in spontaneous letters. It is not very usual for a young person to attribute the discovery of his or her distinctive style of intelligence to an enabling and empowering school or teacher. Judy Logan's students do so. They have a distinctive honesty, integrity, and sense of play which they (and I) attribute in part to her recognition of their lives as persons in their own right, full of real and potential life.

The success stories recounted in this book tie in with and validate most of the major educational reforms in the United States today. Many educators are exhausted by the quantity of school reforms, seeing each as dealing with a new and different problem area, and therefore burdening already overworked educators with ever more "shoulds" and "oughts." I believe that most of the recent education reforms have a generalized coherence which those who developed them (often in competition with each other) didn't see, or didn't admit to seeing. A single chapter in *Teaching Stories* is likely to bring to mind, illustrate, or illuminate, several reforms at once.

Among these are team teaching, collaborative learning, faculty development, attentiveness to learning styles, school restructuring, peer counseling, writing across the disciplines, gender equity, race equity, cooperative learning, alternative assessment, literature-based instruction, multicultural curricula, school/community programming, interdisciplinary study, family life education, global studies, peace studies, hands-on math and science, conflict resolution, parent involvement, values education, and the role of teacher-as-researcher.

In listing these movements and initiatives separately, I depart from the immediacy of *Teaching Stories*, which I see as an important book in late 20th century U.S. educational history precisely because of its syntheses embedded/embodied in stories. The single reforms are the projects of the City of Educational Abstraction. *Teaching Stories* brings it all to life, in Maya Angelou's land of river, rock, and tree, where people and provisioning for our actual journeys of living and dying are at the center of education.

I have said that Judy Logan's teaching implicitly asks of old prohibitions "Why not?" and "What if . . . ?". We know that for many students school is boring, irritating, insulting, or frightening. Yet many teachers have it in them to teach as Logan does. School structures need to give such teachers space to do what they do and share what they know. Like students, teachers need places they want to be in, places which respect their imaginations and knowledge. *Teaching Stories* testifies to some brilliant ways in which we might teach to students' actual human needs and interests. In these stories you can see it happening: the students, the class, the aliveness, the commitment to education as growth and development. Judy Logan is in the picture, but she does not block our view of the students. One editor in rejecting the manuscript wrote that this book "is not about teaching as most of us know it." Exactly, which is why "education as we know it" is in so much trouble.

Year after year, Judy Logan's former students return to visit her. As *Teaching Stories* testifies, they realize how powerfully she worked to enable them to do what they learned to do. In grades six, seven, and eight, however, what they knew most clearly was that they were co-creating the education they were receiving. In retrospect, they value the educator who divined and entered into serious conversation with their own beings. All of this is made clear in the book in language which is candid, poignant, engaging, and alive. Perhaps Logan's style of writing will do for all readers what she does for students—help us to trust ourselves, our voices, our experiences, our own stories in the stream of time.

Peggy McIntosh
Wellesley College Center for Research on Women
Wellesley, Massachusetts, April 1993

Selected Bibliography

Bloom, Benjamin. *Taxonomy of Education Objectives, Handbook I: Cognitive Domain.* New York: David McKay Pulishing Company, 1956.

Eustis, Helen. "A Licking A Boy Could Be Proud Of," from *A Family is a Way of Feeling.* New York: The Macmillan Company, 1966.

Forbes, Kathryn. "Mama and Her Bank Account," from *Mama's Bank Account,* New York: Harcourt, Brace, and World, 1943.

Gregorc, Anthony, *Inside Styles: Beyond the Basics.* Maynard, Mass: Gabriel Systems, 1985.

Hughes, Langston. "Thank You, Ma'am," from A *Family is a Way of Feeling.* New York: The Macmillan Company, 1966.

McIntosh, Peggy. "Interactive Phases of Curricular Re-Vision: a Feminist Perspective, Working Paper No. 124" (1983), and "Interactive Phases of Curricular and Personal Re-Vision With Regard to Race" (1990). Wellesley, MA: Center for Research on Women, Wellesley College, Wellesley, MA 02181

Morgan, Carol McAfee, "Anita's Gift," from A *Family is a Way of Feeling.* New York: The Macmillan Company, 1966.

Rogers, Lilith, "For Angela at Puberty," from *in Lilith Returns.* Sebastopol, CA: Green Snake Press, P.O. Box 2455, 1989.

Rush, Anne Kent. *Moon, Moon.* New York, NY and Berkeley, CA: Random House and Moon Books, 1976.

Saroyan, William. "The Parsley Garden," from *Counterpoint in Literature,* Sacramento, CA: California State Series, 1967.

Style, Emily. "Curriculum as Window and Mirror," from *Listening for All Voices: Gender Balancing the School Curriculum.* New Jersey: Oak Knoll School Monograph, Summit, 1988.

Tavris, Carol and Baumgartner, Dr. Annette I. "How Would Your Life Be Different?" Redbook, 1983.

Taylor, T. Roger. *Building a Quality Program for Gifted Students Resource Handbook.* Paso Robles, CA: Bureau of Education and Research, 1989.

Wright, Richard. "The Streets of Memphis," from *Coping.* New York: The Macmillan Company, 1966.

Acknowledgements

Thank you to Peggy McIntosh for her encouragement, inspiration, assistance, patience, and validation. Thank you to the Center for Research on Women at Wellesley College for their support and to the American Association of University Women for the Eleanor Roosevelt Grant.

A special thank you to Cathy Nelson, who has worked tirelessly on behalf of this book, whose faith in this book from the very beginning is deeply appreciated, and without whom Teaching Stories would not be available. Thank you to the board of directors of the Minnesota Inclusiveness Program for their constant support, and to the Minnesota SEED staff for their love and enthusiasm. Many thanks to Pam Rizzi, whose constant hard work and commitment to meeting all requests is much appreciated.

Thank you to Ellen Boneparth, Willa Cofield, Brenda Flyswithhawks, Nancy Letts, Janice Koch, Emily Style, Dena Randolph and my SEED sisters and brothers for giving me the courage to speak in my own voice, and to Gail Dent for providing me with the comforts of her home to use as a work space. Thank you to my colleagues Kathie Edeli and Frank Foreman, whose dedication to children and commitment to education are a daily inspiration to me. Thank you to the San Francisco chapter of the National Organization for Women, who provided wonderful opportunities for our boys and girls to write about female heroes. Thank you to the many readers who took the time to write and respond to this book.

Thank you to the caretakers who keep me balanced: Lillian Cartwright, Alison Ebata, Morgan Henderson, and Susan Schwartz.

Most of all, thank you to my students, who never stop teaching me, and to their parents, who entrust me with the lives of their children.

About the Author

Judy Logan taught middle school at inner-city public schools in San Francisco for thirty-one years. For twenty-four of those years, she was a teacher in the school where she was once a student, and which her mother, aunts, uncles, sister, and cousin once attended. From her second-floor classroom window she could see the hospital where she was born, her grandmother's home where her mother first brought her as an infant, the back of the house in which she grew up, and the roof of the house in which she now lives.

She has also traveled extensively and has completed courses in women's studies in Kenya, India, Israel, Greece, and Hawaii. She was a mentor teacher for nine years in San Francisco working on multicultural and gender-inclusive curriculum. She is a consultant for the National Seeking Educational Equity and Diversity (SEED) Program and the Minnesota SEED Program.

Now retired from teaching for sixteen years, she works as an educational consultant and lives in San Francisco with two kitties and three rabbits.

Additional copies of *Teaching Stories* may be purchased at www.createspace.com/4275633 or at amazon.com and other online retailers.

42989195R00107

Made in the USA
Charleston, SC
10 June 2015